# not
# my
# plans

# not my plans

## WHEN GOD ALLOWS A PARENT'S WORST FEAR TO COME TRUE

KATHY YOKELEY

In loving memory
of our beautiful Natalie

# acknowledgements

Special thanks to:

Crystal for following the Holy Spirit's prompting and encouraging me to "*write the book.*"

Lizzy for helping me organize my thoughts and for her creative insight.

Jerri for looking over my work and getting me to the finish line.

Will and Meagan for their love and encouragement.

And most of all, Tom, for his steadfast love and for graciously supporting me and keeping things moving on the home front while I "holed up" on the weekends to write.

# contents

## introduction

# a different plan

"You can make many plans,
but the LORD's purpose will prevail."
—Proverbs 19:21 (NLT)

When our only daughter, Natalie, was born, I had all the same hopes and dreams for her that I had for her older brother, Will. Before her birth, I'd miscarried a baby and had a scare early in my pregnancy with her. So when I finally held my precious baby girl in my arms, I assumed her safe arrival meant God planned for her to live a full life here on earth. She'd grow up, go to college, get married, and have children of her own. She'd definitely outlive her father and me.

But God had a different plan for our girl. Natalie was just twelve years old when she was diagnosed with inoperable anaplastic astrocytoma, a cancer that attacks the spinal cord and brain. She fought this dreadful disease courageously for over nine months, never losing hope that she might be healed. Though cancer won the earthly battle just twenty-three days after her thirteenth birthday, Natalie won the war. Despite brutal suffering, she never wavered in her faith in God or her commitment to touch others with God's love. Today she is indeed joyously healed and living a full life for all eternity in heaven with her Lord and Savior Jesus Christ.

Never in my wildest dreams could I have anticipated such a calamity

1

would be in God's plan for my daughter's life. Yet I never doubted God's love during our family's dark walk through cancer. He gave us the strength to push through each day and has kept us afloat when the waves of grief have threatened to overpower us. Since our girl's death, we have experienced daily the beautiful promise given in scripture:

The faithful love of the Lord never ends! His mercies never cease. Great is his faithfulness; his mercies begin afresh each morning. (Lamentations 3:22-23, NLT)

This side of heaven, I will always miss my girl and mourn the events in my life that I will never experience with her. But when I focus on where she is and the wonderful assurance that I will see her again, tears of sadness turn to joy. Natalie left behind such a legacy of impact on others through her courage, kindness, and steadfast faith. It is now my turn to show the courage and faith my daughter demonstrated and to persevere in keeping my focus on the "God hugs"—what I call the blessings along the way—instead of my grief and loss.

It is also my heart's desire to offer to others the immeasurable comfort and hope God has provided me and my family (2 Corinthians 1:3-4). For this reason, I take every opportunity to share Natalie's story, including in this written form. A story that is not just of tragedy and a young life cut painfully short but of God's infinite faithfulness and love.

As you read the following pages, I hope and pray my experiences will offer some insight into the immediate and continuing day-to-day struggles that come with the illness and loss of a child. If you haven't personally experienced devastating loss, then you may find this book useful for future interactions with those who have, and it may help you better understand how to effectively offer them comfort.

Most of all, I pray that through Natalie's story you will see God's faithfulness in your own life circumstances and be drawn closer to him.

# in loving memory

"I will turn their mourning into gladness;
I will give them comfort and joy instead of sorrow."
—Jeremiah 31:13 (NIV)

**Rock Hill, South Carolina, July 2018**

Butterflies stirred in my stomach as I pulled into the parking lot of the Magnolia Room, a lovely wedding venue about thirty miles south of our home in Charlotte, North Carolina. In less than an hour, my only son, Will, would be marrying his sweet bride, Meagan, officially replacing me as the number one girl in his life. He'd soon have a family and home of his own—twelve hours away from us.

*This one is different, Kathy!* I reminded myself sternly. *It hurts to let him go. But this parting isn't permanent.*

The butterflies grew stronger as I headed inside. I wanted everything to be perfect for my son and his bride, and I was nervous to discover how the months of planning had all come together. But the moment I stepped inside the venue's ballroom, I could feel the delighted smile spread across my face. An altar at the front of the room was framed in greenery and flanked by tall arrangements of white hydrangeas and pink peonies. Cream satin drapery curtained the walls, and gold chairs enough to accommodate one-hundred-eighty guests were lined up in equal rows to create an aisle down the middle.

As I perused the room, my eyes fell on a small table directly to my right. Despite the joy of this day, a twinge of sadness twisted inside me. Walking over to inspect it, I knew what I'd find since I'd chosen the items myself earlier that week. Pictures of Will's only sibling, Natalie, stood beside her softball cap, a small album containing scriptures she'd hand-written, a drawing of her, and a few candles. There was also a framed sign that read:

### Natalie

*Although we cannot see you*
*We know you are here*
*Smiling down*
*Watching over us*
*Forever in our hearts*
*Forever in our lives*
*In loving memory*

As I looked over each item, memories flooded my mind—mostly of happier times. Emotion welled up inside me from that deep place where my body can no longer suppress the pain and surrenders to the sobs. Our little girl, who should have been celebrating the happiest day in her brother's life, was here only in spirit, in our memories, and in our hearts.

Tears had pooled in my eyes when I heard someone call out my name. Thankful for the timely distraction, I joined the wedding party now congregating in the foyer. The processional music started. Both sets of grandparents and the mother of the bride were seated. Now it was my turn. *Take a deep breath, Kathy!*

An usher, one of Will's childhood friends, took my arm, and we started down the aisle. As I turned to take my seat on the front row, I saw the empty chair next to mine. A pink long-stemmed rose lay across the chair, accompanied by a sign with Natalie's picture on it and the words *"Reserved, Natalie Yokeley."*

My husband, Tom, was Will's best man, so he was already standing up front with the other groomsmen. I felt a tad melancholy sitting there all by myself until I looked to my right past the empty chair and saw Giovanna, who had been a close friend of Natalie's, sitting in the next seat. My melancholy lifted as we exchanged a smile.

I turned my attention back to the front as Will joined the wedding party. He looked so handsome in his navy tuxedo. Blue has always been my favorite color on him because it contrasts with his blond hair and brings out the beautiful blue in his eyes. Tears welled up again. This time they were the tears of a proud mom.

*Focus, Kathy! Focus, focus, focus! You can't cry through the ceremony. It'll mess up your makeup.*

Now the bridesmaids were entering. As they walked down the aisle in their long aqua-green dresses with matching bouquets, it hit me that in other circumstances Natalie would likely have been one of them. How pretty she would have looked with her dark hair in that particular color of dress.

*Stop, Kathy!* My eyes were filling with water again. I turned my attention back to the groomsmen, forcing my mind to focus on anything but my daughter. It was a defense mechanism that had worked well for me over the past decade.

The Wedding March began, and we all rose to our feet as Meagan appeared with her father in the doorway of the ballroom. She looked stunning with her beautiful brown eyes, olive skin, and dark-brown hair in an elegant upswept style. I managed to get control of my tear ducts as father and daughter made their way down the aisle. Then the ceremony began. My heart swelled with joy and gratitude to my heavenly Father as Will and Meagan pledged their love for each other with God-honoring words.

Then it was time for the scripture reading. Natalie's childhood friend Giovanna had been chosen for this part of the program. Getting to her feet, she walked nervously forward to the microphone. Her voice steadied as she began reading a passage from the New Testament epistle to the Romans.

I am convinced that nothing can ever separate us from God's love. Neither death nor life, neither angels nor demons, neither our fears for today nor our worries about tomorrow … indeed, nothing in all creation will ever be able to separate us from the love of God that is revealed in Christ Jesus our Lord. (Romans 8:38-39, NLT)

As I listened to the beautiful promises of God's love, I suddenly realized, *That child will be in heaven one day because of my daughter.*

Nor will she be the only one.

# family

"'For I know the plans I have for you,' says the Lord.
'They are plans for good and not for disaster,
to give you a future and a hope.'"
—Jeremiah 29:11 (NLT)

As a young girl, I dreamed of getting married and having two kids and a dog. Most girls I've known dream of meeting Prince Charming and having a family just as boys dream of becoming firefighters, professional athletes, and such. But thinking back, I wonder why precisely two kids and a dog. Especially since I grew up in a *large* family with *no* dog. And I never really cared if my hypothetical offspring were boys or girls so long as there were only two.

Maybe subconsciously I wanted one to be the oldest and one the youngest so none were stuck in the middle like me. Growing up, I never really found my place among my four siblings. I wasn't the oldest, the youngest, the smartest, or the athlete.

That's quite possibly how the dog came into play. Dogs make us feel as though we're the most important people on earth. They greet us when we step through the door as if we've been gone for months rather than hours or even minutes. As a child, I desired that kind of attention but seldom felt as if I deserved it. I just didn't believe there was anything special about me.

Now don't get me wrong. I was a happy child and blessed with a great family. When I was two years old, my father's work as an engineer moved us from our extended family in western North Carolina, first to Ohio, then Massachusetts, then Arkansas. So it was just the seven of us, and each new move meant getting used to new schools and making new friends.

My parents were loving, which included discipline when we were defiant. And we were good kids overall, though we did our fair share of bickering with each other—especially when crammed into our yellow, wood-grain Pontiac Grand Safari station wagon, during the twelve-hour drive from Arkansas to North Carolina each summer.

I have countless happy memories of family vacations in the Carolinas. Cookouts with grandparents, aunts, uncles, and cousins included all the burgers, hot dogs, and homemade vanilla ice cream we could eat. Chigger and mosquito bites covered our sweaty little legs as we ran around after dusk chasing lightning bugs and each other. A summer highlight was driving to the South Carolina coast to play on a sandy beach and bob up and down in the ocean waves.

While afforded much opportunity as children, we weren't spoiled by any means. My mother was able to stay home with us during the day, which she did until my youngest siblings started school, and then she took a part-time job at the local J.C. Penney department store. We were allowed, and even encouraged, to participate in activities like sports, band, and Scouts, but we were also expected to complete our household chores. Birthdays were celebrated in a simple but special manner—Mom would bake our favorite cake, mine being cherry chip.

My parents taught us the importance of good manners, hard work, and being responsible. They also modeled the importance of faith in God. I'm pretty sure we were in attendance at the various churches we went to with each new move every time the doors opened. My parents were actively involved, even serving as Sunday school teachers. But church had a big, impersonal feel to me, and I wasn't an outgoing child, so I dreaded going.

# family

My perception of God became a reflection of how I felt being in church, which was that I was unable to measure up. While the churches we attended were solid in biblical truth, I don't recall hearing much about God's grace when I was young. So I only knew God as someone to fear. I thought that people who *didn't* measure up to God's standards—i.e., sinned—went to hell. Maybe that's not exactly how it was worded, but that's what I heard.

I did accept Jesus Christ as my Savior when I was eight years old. But at the time it was more out of fear of going to hell than understanding what it meant to be a disciple of Jesus. As a result, I wasn't drawn to having a close personal relationship with God until decades later. Instead, I became distracted by what the outside world deemed important—social activities, good grades, material things.

I had a similar fear of not measuring up in school. My parents placed a high value on our academics, but my dad especially pushed us to rise to our full potential. I was a good student, but I didn't always get the highest grade, and I never wanted to disappoint him. A bright man and high achiever, Dad worked hard and was promoted throughout the years but never at the expense of his family. He demonstrated a healthy work-life balance; he almost always had dinner with us, was at our evening events, and spent time with us on the weekends.

Family was important to my parents and the reason for our final move when I was fifteen. Their announcement that we were moving to South Carolina was a tough pill to swallow, especially since I was just starting high school and wanted to stay with my friends. I was too young then to understand my parents' desire to live closer to their own elderly parents and help care for them. All I cared about was that they were ruining my life!

We pulled into the driveway of our new split-level home in Rock Hill, South Carolina, on a cold January evening. I couldn't sleep that night. I was too anxious about attending a new school the next morning. I've never liked change and had no idea what to expect. When I'd changed schools in Arkansas, it had been the normal transitions from elementary to middle school to high school, and I'd always had my friends there to navigate new waters together. This was a new environment I'd have to figure out all by myself.

But the biggest challenge in my young life actually proved to be a pivotal time for me. Not only did God develop a strength and confidence in me that might have gone untapped had I stayed in my Arkansas comfort zone, but unbeknownst to me someone special resided less than an hour away.

A few months later, I turned sixteen and started my first job at Carowinds, a nearby theme park I'd visited as a child. I viewed this opportunity only as a means to an end so I could buy clothes and fund my social life. But it turned out to be much more significant than I could ever have imagined.

I was working the summer season after high school graduation to save for college when an *unpleasant* incident one afternoon led to a very *pleasant* encounter. Some kids were being reckless on the ride I was supervising. In trying to keep them from hurting themselves and others, I badly twisted my left ankle. I sat on the hard asphalt, trying to push back tears, while a medic checked out my foot. I was exhausted and perspiring from working all day in the sweltering August heat, and my embarrassment over my sweaty, smelly socks and feet was almost as severe as the throbbing pain in my ankle. All I wanted was to go home, shower off the grit, and climb into bed.

But when a good-looking blonde park security officer named Tom showed up, my rush to get home slowed a bit. Park protocol dictated he accompany me to the park's first aid station. He proved to be a chatty, funny conversationalist, and I appreciated him taking my mind off the pain while we waited for the doctor. I found out that this was his summer job too, and he would soon be heading back to college for his senior year.

I had to go into the examining room alone. When I emerged with my diagnosis—a sprained ankle—Tom had already returned to his security duties. Since the summer was almost over, the sprained ankle put an end to my job at the park. But it wasn't a total loss as God had just introduced me to my future husband.

# family

I returned to work at the park following my freshman year of college. Tom was back there as well for the summer, and we started dating a few weeks before I left for my sophomore year of college. He graduated shortly after and took a job as a logistics specialist in his hometown of Charlotte, North Carolina. Though we now lived several hours apart, we managed to maintain a healthy long-distance relationship for the next three years. Two months after I received my Bachelor of Arts in Journalism from the University of South Carolina, we married and settled in Charlotte.

Neither of us wanted children right away, so we bought a town home, did a little traveling, and focused on our careers—he in the field of logistics and me as an advertising professional. I'd accomplished my principal goals—a college degree, marriage, starting my career, buying a house. But as with high school, those dreams were consumed with attaining material things, not spiritual. God knew he wasn't my priority.

Despite a lack of interest on my part, God kept pursuing me. And his pursuit was not in vain. Like me, Tom had attended church growing up and had accepted Christ as his Savior at the age of sixteen. Now as young married adults, Tom and I began worshipping at a local church. This started out more like an obligation than a desire to be a part of a church community again. My parents had instilled in me a foundation of faith and churchgoing, so to me this was just what adults did. You worked five days a week. Then on Sunday, you went to church.

But I still didn't really understand God's love for me. My default frame of reference was that if you did something wrong, God would be angry and punish you. And yet, though still somewhat apprehensive of God, I felt strangely drawn to him. Tom and I waded into church waters, but we weren't quite ready to fully submerge ourselves, so we kept our church engagement at arm's length.

Five years into our marriage, we were ready to start a family. Tom came from a family of four, just as I'd once dreamed of having, and he also wanted only two children, so we were on the same page. We traded our town home for a house with a yard. Nine months later, we welcomed our son, Will, into our home and hearts.

It was then that something happened inside me. I yearned for my little boy to know the Bible stories I'd learned as a child and to experience what I'd experienced spiritually. This necessitated more than just showing up for an hour of worship each week. Tom and I became increasingly involved in our church.

Three and a half years later, our daughter, Natalie, became the fourth and final human member of our family. As our kids grew, so did my trust in God. I joined a mothers' prayer group and a women's Bible study. For the first time in my life, I wasn't just learning *about* God but actually wanted to *know* him. After decades in church, I finally understood my place in God's family, and I made a renewed commitment to follow Jesus Christ as my Savior.

Natalie was six, Will going on ten one cold November afternoon in 2001 when our neighbor, on school carpool duty that day, pulled her minivan into our driveway. Jumping out of the van, the kids ran toward me. They'd been eagerly wishing the school day away so they could get home, and I was just as excited to share what I held in my hands—a four-week-old Miniature Dachshund puppy.

His tiny black body with accents of brown on his paws, nose, and underbelly fit easily into my cupped palms. Taking one look, Will commented, "He looks just like the mouse from my book."

The book in question was *Cricket in Times Square*, which was about animal friends Chester the Cricket, Harry the Cat, and Tucker the Mouse. We'd already picked out a name in anticipation of our puppy's arrival, but we all agreed he did indeed look more like a Tucker than a Snickers. Tucker the Miniature Dachshund was now officially a member of our family, and the perfect home I'd dreamed of as a child with two parents, two kids, and a dog was now complete.

This was one of the happiest, most fulfilling decades of my life personally, professionally, and spiritually. In fact, I just wanted to freeze time and keep things exactly as they were. But God had other plans. And little did we know then that an unseen enemy lurked within our family until it suddenly surfaced, altering the course of our lives.

3

# our girl

"Don't let anyone think less of you because you are young.
Be an example to all believers in what you say, in the way
you live, in your love, your faith, and your purity."
—1 Timothy 4:12 (NLT)

N atalie made her debut into this world and into our hearts on November 1, 1995. When the doctor handed her to me, I remember being struck by how fragile she seemed. Will had weighed eight pounds, three ounces at birth. At exactly six pounds, Natalie felt as breakable as a porcelain doll. She also looked very different from her blond-haired, blue-eyed brother with her dark hair and huge, greenish-brown eyes.

My mom took one look at her and laughed. "You prayed those eyes into her!"

It was true I'd always wanted my daughter, if I had one, to have big eyes because I always considered my own rather small. As I examined each feature on her small, round face, I was filled with a sense of awe at how God makes such amazing creatures.

Natalie's infancy was pretty routine until she was about two months old, when she started running a fever with no apparent cause. After a spinal tap to rule out meningitis, her pediatrician determined she had a urinary tract infection. This was our first serious health scare as parents, and I experienced my first extreme "momma bear" moment. All I wanted was to shield my daughter from the pain, and I'd take on anyone threatening her well-being. Thankfully, antibiotics cleared up the infection, and we settled back into our "let's figure this out as we go" parenting routine.

Three and a half when Natalie was born, Will doted on his baby sister. If I was out of the room when she cried, he'd run to get me. From the beginning, their personalities were as different as their appearance. Will was more extroverted and even-keeled. Natalie was more strong-willed and introverted. She hated being the center of attention. If I put a bow in her hair and someone commented on how pretty she looked, she'd reach up and pull it out. And she was painfully shy except with people she knew well.

One evening when she was three or four, Natalie and I were at the ballpark waiting for Will's Little League baseball team to start their game. A friend of mine whose son was also on Will's team had joined us to watch the game. Pulling out some candy to snack on, she offered Natalie a piece. As my daughter took the candy, I instructed, "Natalie, honey, you need to say thank you."

Natalie just stared at us, so I repeated, "Honey, you need to say thank you."

Again, she stared, not as though being defiant but more as though she just couldn't get the words to come out. I continued a little more firmly, "If you can't say thank you, then you can't have the candy."

Immediately, Natalie lifted her small hand with the candy tucked inside and handed it back to my friend. She'd rather miss out on a treat than talk to an adult outside her close family circle.

Natalie's facial expressions often said more than her words. Her engaging smile went all the way to her eyes. As mentioned, her eyes were big and beautiful, and she knew how to work them! In fact, she could have been a model for the eye-roll emoji. Any time someone said or did something ridiculous, her eyes went into high gear. I didn't dare look her way at times for fear of bursting out laughing at an inopportune moment.

Her eyes sent a different message when she was sad. The anguish in their greenish-brown depths was so vivid it could break your heart.

Once when she was a toddler, she fell on the driveway and needed stitches in her forehead. Wrapping her papoose-style in a blanket, the doctor asked me to hold her down while he did the sutures. Till then I'd been trying to be strong for her. But I almost fell apart when her big, sad eyes looked up at me as if to say, "Mommy, why are you letting them do this to me?"

Of course, when Natalie was mad, she didn't have to say a word. When she was in kindergarten, parents were allowed to visit the school to have lunch with their child. On one particular day, Tom had arranged to meet Natalie for lunch. This entailed the student sitting at a special table and even inviting another friend along, so it was a big occasion for a kindergartner. But space at the special table was limited, and Tom was late for their "date." When Tom arrived, Natalie had taken her seat at her regular class table. Tom did manage to take a commemorative photo, but if looks could kill! I still laugh every time I see that photo.

Though an introvert, Natalie's go-getter personality made her more open to trying new things than Will, my cautious one. When she was five and Will eight-and-a-half, *she* finally coaxed *him* into riding a roller-coaster. Once on the roller-coaster, she was the one yelling at the top of her lungs and waving her hands in the air while Will gripped the safety bar with white knuckles.

With her powerful will, Natalie definitely tried my patience. When she set her mind on something, getting her to change course meant a fierce battle, and she could quickly figure out some way to get what she wanted. I tried weaning her off her pacifier by cutting off the tip, a tactic that had worked successfully for Will.

She just looked at me as if to say, "I'll show you!" Then she put the pacifier back in her mouth, stuck her tongue into the tip, and somehow managed to achieve suction. As I stood there dumbfounded, I thought, *Ugh, child! This personality trait is not going to serve you well in life!*

But her determination also helped her push through difficult situations. Four months before starting kindergarten, she tried to kick a soccer ball while standing on a trampoline. Her leg came down at the wrong angle, and she broke her femur. She immediately begged, "Mommy, please don't let them put a cast on me!"

Unfortunately, the emergency room doctor informed us she'd be getting a spica cast. This started at her midsection, traveled down her left leg to her ankle, and down her right leg to the top of her knee with a bar connecting the legs. For the next nine weeks, including much of that summer, Natalie had to lie on her back in the body cast. If this wasn't bad enough, the cast was a deep red, not exactly the color of choice for a child who hated people looking at her.

During this ordeal, my mom decided that Natalie needed a bell so she could ring it when she wanted me. Like any young child, Natalie rang the bell incessantly. One day while I was trying to complete a project, she kept ringing the bell. I finally walked into her room and pleaded, "Natalie, I will pay you ten dollars if you can go just thirty minutes without saying 'Mommy!'"

With a sly grin, she nodded agreement. As soon as I walked out into the hallway, I heard her sweet, little voice calling, "Kaaa-thy!" She did not get her ten dollars!

For the entire time Natalie was in her cast, we pulled her around to all of Will's baseball games, church, PTA, and other meetings in a little red wagon. Natalie adamantly insisted we conceal her cast with a blanket whenever we left the house. She had to be roasting hot under the blanket, but all she cared about was that the cast be covered up so no one could see it.

Once the cast came off, her legs were too weak to carry her, so Natalie had to use crutches until she regained her strength. She absolutely hated the crutches and was determined not to use them during an upcoming family beach trip. Like a toddler learning to walk, she began crawling around and pulling herself up on chairs. By the time we left for the beach, she was walking on her own.

When Natalie started kindergarten two months later, we were heading out the door for her first day when she abruptly paused. With a serious expression on her face, she asked, "You don't really expect me to spend the best years of my life in school, do you?"

I had to laugh before breaking it to her that she would indeed be spending much of the next years in school. Natalie had a strong scholastic bent and eventually tested into the school's academically gifted program. She wasn't just book smart but intuitive. Maybe because she was so inquisitive. She paid close attention to what was happening around her, and her brain seemed to be engaged every waking moment.

Tom called her my mini-me, and indeed she was in many ways like me with similar thought processes. Like Natalie, I tended toward being analytical and liked to take what I knew and think on it before making decisions. I recently found an award she received from her fifth-grade teacher that read, "Given in recognition of your unique talent to analyze and think outside the box in order to achieve greater insight and understanding for yourself and others."

But Natalie's shyness continued to plague her. In school, she simply could not muster the courage to speak or read compositions in front of classmates. Tom and I decided that being involved in group sports might help her develop confidence. She wanted no part of soccer after her leg injury and was equally uninterested in gymnastics. When she was seven years old, we tried softball. That proved a hit and became her passion.

Being part of an all-girls team with a common goal to cheer each other on helped Natalie feel more comfortable in a group setting. Over the years of playing together, they all became close friends. A caring teacher also helped her overcome her anxiety at reading and talking in front of others.

But while Natalie didn't crave the limelight, she often drew attention simply because she was so funny. From very young, she loved telling corny jokes and making others laugh. "Why did the cookie go to the hospital? Because it felt crummy! Why couldn't the pony sing a lullaby? She was a little horse!"

Whether intentional or not, her commentary on life was often humorous. One day when we drove by a local church, she inquired about a Divorce Care banner hanging outside. I did my best to explain such a complex topic in a way a ten-year-old could grasp. As several silent moments passed, I was unsure how well I'd succeeded. Then Natalie's sweet, little voice spoke up. "Well, you never know when you're going to latch onto a loser!"

Natalie had no interest in conforming to clothing styles or fads. She liked to be neat but comfortable. When we shopped, she'd pick what she liked, not the latest Abercrombie & Fitch or whatever else was the rage for her age group. Nor was she interested in popularity. She wanted to hang around with people she liked and refused to do or say unkind things just to be part of the popular girls clique. Though an introvert by nature, she spoke up forthrightly if she had a strong opinion on a topic or saw someone being treated poorly.

The summer before middle school, the church youth group had an outing to a water park. Natalie brought along one of her friends. As they waited their turn to descend a particularly steep waterslide, a boy in front of them refused to take the plunge. Natalie's friend immediately began taunting him. Natalie told the other girl she wasn't being nice and asked how she'd feel if someone embarrassed her like that. She then assured the boy there was nothing wrong with changing his mind and going back down the stairs.

It wasn't Natalie who recounted this story to us but the boy's mom, one of the group chaperones who'd arrived at the top of the slide just as this incident was happening. Once her son decided against going down the slide, Natalie turned those big, expressive eyes and smile on the chaperone. "But *you* will be the coolest counselor ever if you go down!"

"It cost me a giant wedgie to take that plunge!" the boy's mom told us later. "But how could I resist that challenge?"

Being an introvert, Natalie preferred spending time with one person as opposed to a group and was discerning about who she allowed into her small circle of friends. But she also showed concern for those who needed a friend or helping hand. As a fourth-grader, she took a neighborhood kindergartner under her wing because he was intimidated by riding the school bus. When a class assignment required pairing off, her sixth-grade English teacher told us how Natalie would choose someone who didn't have a friend to work with or who needed extra help.

As a family we'd always been actively involved in our church, and when she was ten, Natalie shared with us her decision to accept Jesus as her Lord and Savior. It wasn't until much later that we learned the full extent of how she'd shared her faith in God with her school friends. She was not shy about voicing strong opinions, whether about her faith or what was happening around her. But her friends also knew they could count on her to love them unconditionally. Years later when Sydney, Natalie's best friend since first grade, was in college, she wrote to me about her memories of Natalie.

Natalie was always the friend who was the most honest. If you were doing something you weren't supposed to, she would call you out. If she didn't like you, she would tell you. If she thought something was cool, she would tell you. I think the best quality Nat had was that she was so real. She knew the value of friendship and never let me down.

Natalie met Giovanna, who later read the scripture passage at Will and Meagan's wedding, when they were both in sixth grade. Natalie helped Giovanna navigate some situations with girls who were being mean, and the two became close friends. As a college junior, Giovanna wrote:

Natalie led by example, visibly showing me that people and their opinions do not identify us. She constantly reminded me not to worry about what others had to say. She shared God's love with me every day and encouraged me to do my best no matter what. She inspired me to trust the Lord during tough times and reminded me that our strength came from him.

Geneva was another close friend since kindergarten when the two girls joined the same Sunday school class. Their birthdays were just one week apart, and since they attended the same church and even the same school in later elementary, they remained good friends right up to

Natalie's death. Eight years after Natalie passed away, Geneva shared her thoughts.

As we got older, there were more facets to our friendship than just being in the same class. People could be mean and rude, excluding people based on surface characteristics. But not Natalie. She was genuine and kind to everyone she encountered. I didn't realize it at the time, but this distinction was important for me personally because I was becoming lost in discovering how to present myself and feel comfortable in my own skin. Natalie discouraged my judging of people, and she pointed out to me when I was being rude to others. These are qualities rarely found in most adults today, and for her to be cognizant of this at her age is nothing short of a miracle. Natalie was a responsible, levelheaded, intelligent, mindful, caring, kind, and overall amazing individual. She had incredible intuition and a strong handle on what it meant to be a wonderful human. She was compassionate, empathetic, sympathetic, friendly, and welcoming. She never gave up on you.

# togetherness

"Finally, all of you, be like-minded,
be sympathetic, love one another,
be compassionate and humble."
—1 Peter 3:8 (NIV)

Natalie developed more confidence with each passing year. But I saw the biggest change between elementary and middle school. When I attended her sixth-grade parent-teacher conferences, one teacher told me Natalie was the one he could depend on whenever he needed a volunteer. My flabbergasted expression must have communicated my thought. *Are you sure we are talking about my child?*

Natalie could also use her charm and gift of persuasion to her own advantage. Since she and I shared many similarities in temperament, I could better resist her tactics. But she had Tom wrapped around her finger from an early age. He admits, "She could sweet-talk me into getting her almost anything she wanted."

I recently found a note Natalie had written when she was eight that brought a touch of sadness but also made me laugh. Based on how the note begins, it was undoubtedly one of those moments when she'd been reprimanded for her behavior and was trying to work her charm on me with a compliment.

Mom, I know you are mad at me right now. Me and Will are watching *Family Feud*, and Will said we should go to California one day and go on the show because of the knowledge in our family, mostly from you. So we were wondering if we could go there some day. Can we? Well you don't have to decide now, and if I go on it, I have to wait until I'm old enough, but it's something we can think about. I hope you will forgive me. I love you, Natalie

In her P.S., she'd included the phone number for the game show. Without knowing what was on the horizon, I'd kept the note because I found it so endearing.

When Will and Natalie were small, I was more engaged with their school and other activities since Tom's job as an international logistics specialist meant a hectic schedule and long hours, with requests coming in and situations needing dealt with from time zones all over the planet. Before Will's birth, I'd been working full-time in the advertising department at a local soft drink bottler. Thankfully, I was blessed with a family-oriented boss who let me work from home half-days once Will was born, a privilege I didn't take for granted.

By the time Natalie came along three and half years later, Will was in a preschool class in the mornings, but I still cherished our time together in the afternoons. Once he started kindergarten, my flexible work schedule allowed me to help out in his classroom once a week and serve on the PTA board. But though I continued to enjoy my work, I also wanted the freedom to be even more involved in my children's constantly varying schedules and activities.

I began praying over whether to quit my job outright or pursue more flexible opportunities. God answered in a way I never expected, opening the door for me to start my own company. Being self-employed with a home office allowed me to remain immersed in my career field while being readily available to the kids. With my newfound flexibility, I could be actively engaged in Will's school while introverted Natalie could tag along at her own comfort level, becoming familiar with the school staff and halls she'd walk one day.

I was so blown away and appreciative of what God had done for me. When I think of this blessing, a Bible verse from the New Testament epistle of Ephesians always comes to my mind:

Now all glory to God, who is able, through his mighty power at work within us, to accomplish infinitely more than we might ask or think. (Ephesians 3:20, NLT)

As I approached my fortieth birthday, I was thoroughly content with how my life was going both at home and the office. Change was certainly not on my mind when I began feeling a strong pull toward Christian ministry. In the spring of 2004, a communications position opened up with a global evangelistic ministry headquartered in Charlotte. Tom and I prayed about it, and God gave us a clear leading that I should accept the position.

We also decided that Tom should quit his job to stay home so the kids wouldn't have to change their routine, which included walking home from the bus stop on school days. Natalie was now in second grade while Will was in middle school, so they attended different schools. This meant they arrived at the bus stop on different buses a good two hours apart. With Charlotte's high crime rate, we wanted to make sure one of us would always be there to meet them.

Tom continued working part-time for several months while he trained his replacement. One day he was late leaving his office, so he wasn't at the bus stop when Natalie's bus arrived. As he turned into our neighborhood, he spotted Natalie already beginning the short trek from the bus stop to our house. Pulling his vehicle alongside her, he said, "Hop in, Nat!"

Natalie just kept walking, face forward. Tom continued pleading with her to get in. But she continued resolutely down the driveway and into the house. Once inside, she looked at him with disappointment in her eyes. "You were late! You know it's not safe for me to walk home by myself!"

Of course, Tom felt awful and immediately tried to make amends by offering to get her favorite treat once her homework was completed. But while Tom's tardiness may have actually scared Natalie, it wasn't just about being safe. Being there to meet her at the bus stop was her time to enjoy our undivided attention, and her daddy not being there had genuinely hurt her. The time Tom and Natalie spent together each afternoon strengthened their already tight-knit bond.

Tom was always ready to be his little girl's hero. In March 2005, our family arrived in Honolulu, Hawaii, for a week's vacation. Natalie was nine at the time, Will almost thirteen; and though I'd done their packing for the trip, Natalie had decided to repack her own suitcase.

Exhausted from the travel and time change, we took a cab straight to the hotel, ate room service, and crashed for the night. It wasn't until the next morning that we discovered a major category of clothing missing from Natalie's suitcase—underwear. Since we didn't have a rental car, we couldn't drive to any retail outlet that might sell little girl's panties.

"I packed your bag because I know what you need," I admonished. "Now you're just going to have to wash the underwear you have on every day."

For the next three nights, Natalie washed her panties in the bathroom sink. Then her soft-hearted daddy helped her blow them dry with the hotel hairdryer. They finally got a reprieve when we found a three-pack of panties at a local children's store. That was our strong-willed girl—doing the punishment for the crime with her daddy at her side helping out!

Though Natalie and Tom were close, our daughter desired quality time with everyone she loved. Spending time together as a family or one-on-one with friends was a top priority for her. This especially included her big brother. Natalie played recreational softball, and Will played baseball. They loved tossing the softball in the yard, and Will helped her with her technique. As a family, we've always been big Atlanta Braves fans, since I have extended family who live there. When we'd visit Atlanta, we'd go see them play, and Will and Natalie would sit for hours together watching their televised games.

They were both extremely competitive at video games, and Natalie would cry when she didn't win. They jumped on the trampoline, played pool, swam at the neighborhood pool, and rode bikes together. Vacations were fun and easy because they entertained each other—and us. I remember one Christmas season when Natalie walked around the house as a videographer while Will narrated a story for us in what he considered to be an Australian accent. It went on for about forty-five minutes, but it's still a family favorite.

They both had nicknames for each other. Since there were two Wills in his fifth-grade class, Will always signed his name Will Y, so Natalie started calling him Willy. And since Natalie was small but tough, Will started calling her Short Iron, later abbreviated to Shorty. Neither minded their nicknames, and I know Natalie quite liked hers because I've found many of her doodles using the name.

By the time Will was fifteen, he'd spurted to over six feet in height while Natalie at three-and-a-half years younger was still well under five feet tall. One Friday night, we'd gone out as a family to a favorite restaurant. We were heading back to our car when Will tapped Natalie on the shoulder. "Bet you can't catch me, Shorty!"

He took off running wildly through the parking lot. Natalie chased after him, shouting, "We'll see who's short when you're on the ground and I'm on top of you!"

We all laughed so hard, not only at her clever quip but the contrast between our petite little dark-haired daughter and her towering blonde big brother. Though small in stature, Natalie had a big presence. She adored her big brother, and he always looked out for her. I thanked him once for spending so much time with her.

"I always want Nat to know I have her back," he answered simply.

Natalie also liked to mother Will, which was humorous considering their age difference, not to mention a good fifteen inches in height. She'd remind him not to drive with earbuds in. Or she'd offer unsolicited advice on his school projects, which he graciously tolerated. She wasn't trying to be bossy, but she knew her big brother didn't have her eye for details and always wanted to help him.

One day Will and a classmate were at our house working on a student council project. Once the classmate left, Natalie gave Will a firm look. "Bring your project down here and let me see it."

Being a kind soul, Will obliged. Natalie gave him some pointers on how to make his project more visually attractive. She also advised him to at the very least straighten out his headline. Though he listened good-naturedly, I assumed his little sister's lecture had gone in one ear and out the other. But the following year after Natalie had passed away, Will asked to show Tom and me his final student council project. It warmed my heart to see his sister's suggestions incorporated into his poster. If she were still with us today, I suspect she'd still be offering Will her nuggets of wisdom.

Natalie also jumped at opportunities to go places with me. When I headed for the door on Saturdays to run errands, I'd hear a little voice piping up behind me. "Where are you going?"

Any adult who has been on a mission to get shopping done with as little aggravation and time expended as possible knows how bringing a child along slows down the process. I'd do my best to convince Natalie of the fun associated with staying home compared to the drudgery of going with me. But she didn't care. She just loved to get out and go.

Eventually we'd head out, grabbing our favorite frozen drinks from a nearby coffee shop on the way. We always enjoyed our time together. With Natalie, conversation was never dull, and her negotiating skills were masterful if she thought she could finagle me into purchasing her something. But she was also okay if she didn't get what she wanted. She'd simply give it "the old college try" and move on when it was clear her efforts were futile.

Natalie was also an avid people watcher. Since I enjoy this too, we had some entertaining conversations about the people and interactions we witnessed together. Her "love language" was quality time,[1] so I knew she needed her mommy-time, and I needed my Nat-time just as much.

But Natalie didn't just go shopping with me. She wanted to be involved in whatever I was doing, even if it was volunteering at church or school. When she was eight, I was part of a Bible study where the author suggested writing down scripture verses as a memory aid and quick reference. Natalie asked if she could help me, so we made it an art project. We bought a couple of small photo albums and some index cards. Decorating our albums, we wrote out verses on the cards and placed them inside.

We also spent time discussing the meaning of the verses and praying together. Chatting about what I was learning through my Bible studies and what she was learning in Sunday school became a natural part of our conversation.

Natalie didn't view herself as someone to be looked up to. Once when she was ten, she and I ran into one of Will's coaches after a baseball game. The coach spent a good amount of time telling us how nice Will was. In fact, we consistently heard these kinds of comments from Will's teachers, classmates, and coaches.

When the coach was done, Natalie looked up at me and commented, "I'll never be as nice as Will."

I understood what she was feeling as her big brother had set a high bar and it certainly must have been daunting to know people would expect the same of her. I looked down into her sweet, little face. "You already are, Peanut. After all, he's got a three-year head start on you. Believe me, when he was your age, he wasn't always nice. Don't you remember how he used to do his best to bug you?"

It was true that Natalie was already exhibiting kindness and deep concern for others beyond her years. She made sure Tom and I felt loved and appreciated by crafting holiday cards and offering nonmonetary gifts such as coupons to do our chores for us. One of my most treasured possessions is the family scrapbook she made for me the last Christmas we spent together. She frequently gave encouraging handwritten notes to us and her friends. On her close friend's tenth birthday, Natalie wanted her to feel celebrated. "Natalie came over to surprise Cameran since I did not have a birthday party for her," her mom recounted. "I still have that birthday banner she brought over for decorations! And we probably still have the Littlest Pet Shop gift that she gave to Cameran." Our tenderhearted girl always wanted others to know they mattered.

Natalie loved deeply and was deeply loved. Although her time here on earth was short, she left a lasting mark on all of us who knew her and eventually on some who never met her. She may have been ill-equipped for our trip to Hawaii that year. But she was well-prepared for her final destination!

5

# the battle begins

"We can rejoice, too, when we run into problems and trials,
for we know that they help us develop endurance.
And endurance develops strength of character, and
character strengthens our confident hope of salvation.
And this hope will not lead to disappointment.
For we know how dearly God loves us, because he has
given us the Holy Spirit to fill our hearts with his love."
—Romans 5:3-5 (NLT)

Natalie had just turned twelve when our nightmare began in January 2008. We'd moved to a new neighborhood of Charlotte, so she'd started sixth grade at a different middle school than the majority of her elementary school peers. Despite missing her elementary school friends and having to adjust to new people and surroundings, she'd done well academically and athletically in her first semester at the new school. Her recreational softball team had just won the fall championship, and she was forming some solid new friendships.

Not long after New Year's, Natalie began complaining that her back hurt. Her complaint came and went, and she seemed fine otherwise, so we didn't think much of it. But when she began struggling to have bowel movements, we decided it was time for her to see a doctor.

The pediatrician concluded that the backache was likely caused by the heavy book bag Natalie carried during the school day. As to the constipation, she'd just returned from a church youth group ski trip up into the Appalachian Mountains north of Charlotte, and the doctor felt she was probably just experiencing a lack of fiber. His prescription was to give her foods that typically promote bowel movement. This worked, and for several weeks everything seemed okay.

Then on Saturday, February 9, I took Natalie and her closest friend, Sydney, to a movie. When Natalie complained that her left leg and buttock felt tingly, I assumed it was caused by sitting still for several hours. But when Natalie woke up the next morning, she couldn't urinate.

In retrospect, all these things happening in a cluster should have been a red flag. But Natalie had always been a healthy child and had passed her wellness checkup with flying colors just a few months earlier. She didn't drink a lot of liquids so she didn't normally empty her bladder often. I handed her a bottle of water as we headed out the door to church, and by the time we arrived she had no problem urinating.

That afternoon, Natalie and I went shopping at the mall. My nonchalance turned to concern when I noticed that she kept falling behind while we were walking. I finally had to put my arm around her to support her weight so she could walk back to the car. As soon as the pediatric practice opened the next morning, Tom called for an emergency appointment. The attending pediatrician was a doctor we hadn't seen before. When he asked her to bend over and touch her toes, she couldn't. He was concerned she might have a problem with her sciatic nerve or possibly scoliosis and recommended an MRI (magnetic resonance imaging) scan later in the week.

That evening I was praying for Natalie as I exercised on my treadmill. My hope and prayer was that the diagnosis would just be a pinched sciatic nerve as scoliosis could mean enduring a back brace during some of the most brutal peer years of a young person's life. Natalie was already making the best of being in a different school than the majority of her friends, and I couldn't bear the thought of the unwanted attention and potential ridicule a back brace might draw.

Just then, the phone rang. If I'd known what was to come, I'd have taken that hypothetical back brace in a second!

Tom picked up the phone. The caller turned out to be the new doctor Natalie had seen earlier in the day. Something about his examination of Natalie had been nagging at him all afternoon, so he'd reached out to a neurologist who'd suggested we take Natalie immediately to the hospital for an MRI.

Maybe we should have wondered why he was suddenly so urgent when he'd been so calm earlier in the day. But to this point the only health issues we'd experienced as parents were Natalie's broken leg and a urinary tract infection in her infancy, a broken wrist and minor asthma attacks for Will, and stitches for both kids. So our minds were simply not in a place where we ever dreamed it could be anything life-threatening.

Will, who was almost sixteen now and a sophomore in high school, was at baseball practice with no way for us to reach him. So I stayed behind to wait for his return while Tom took Natalie for the MRI. We were expecting the whole family to be home together by bedtime. But the full-body MRI took more than two hours, and it was after midnight by the time the neurologist emerged into the waiting room to talk to Tom. My husband had anticipated driving Natalie home as soon as the MRI was finished. So he was caught flat-footed when the neurologist informed him that he'd admitted Natalie to the hospital immediately following the MRI.

Tom called me from the nurses' station to relay his discussion with the doctor. "The MRI showed she has a large mass in her spine. They aren't sure what it is."

I could hear his deep concern in the shaking of his voice, so I asked, "Do you want me to come over? Will's asleep and should be fine for a few hours alone."

"No, she's sleeping now, and the doctor won't be back until morning. Just stay put for now and come over first thing in the morning."

Once I hung up the phone, I returned to my prayers, pleading, "Please, God, don't let anything serious be wrong!"

I got little if any sleep that night. I doubt Tom got much either. I kept telling myself, *Don't borrow trouble, Kathy. It may not be a tumor.*

As soon as I got Will off to school the next morning, I rushed over to the hospital. As parents, we'd never been this scared, but we were also somewhat in shock. We tried to remain cheerful as we waited with Natalie in her room. About mid-morning, a doctor walked in and introduced himself as an oncologist assigned to Natalie's case.

That's when the nightmare started to get real. I felt such a sense of panic but tried to remain outwardly calm for Natalie's benefit as we spoke with the doctor. My earlier fears were confirmed as the mass they'd found on the MRI was indeed a tumor. Like most tumors, a biopsy would determine if it was malignant or benign. It felt like everything was happening at warp speed, and my contented, peaceful world was suddenly spinning out of control. *Our child was having a little trouble with constipation, and now she may have cancer?*

The biopsy was done the very next morning—Wednesday, February 13. After the procedure, the neurosurgeon and oncologist both came to the waiting room to update us. The surgeon explained that he could typically differentiate between a tumor and the spinal cord, then asked, "Do you know what tapioca pudding is?"

I immediately caught his visualization since tapioca differs from regular pudding due to the countless small pearl-like balls of sago starch it contains. When Tom and I both nodded, the surgeon continued: "Natalie's tumor is like tapioca pudding magnified a million times over—little specks of tumor interspersed with her spinal cord all the way from her T2 vertebra to T12."

The upper body spine is made up of twelve thoracic vertebrae, labeled T1-T12, sandwiched in between the cervical vertebrae that make up the neck and the lumbar vertebrae of the lower spine. The surgeon's description meant that Natalie's tumor covered all but the lowest of her thoracic vertebrae. It was the largest such tumor he'd ever seen and because of its scope, inoperable. He'd been concerned about aggravating the tumor, so he'd taken out the smallest amount possible to allow for an accurate biopsy.

My fear intensified as the neurosurgeon continued speaking, and for the first time it began sinking in that my daughter could possibly die. *My child has a huge tumor consuming her spinal cord, and it can't be removed from her body.*

But I was also increasingly angry and hurt at the stark manner in which the surgeon was explaining Natalie's condition. For Tom and me, she was one of the two most important people in our small world. But he spoke as though Natalie was just one more task on his list for the day. He could have been describing the weather rather than a child facing a life-threatening illness. Even the oncologist was angry at the blunt manner in which he'd delivered the news.

But at least we now had some idea what we were facing. While Natalie remained in the post-anesthesia care unit, we returned to her room to begin our wait for the biopsy results. We were told it would take two days to find out whether the tumor was benign or malignant. Why Natalie needed to remain in the hospital was never explained, and since we'd never known anyone who'd had a biopsy, we didn't think to ask. Maybe they were concerned about the tumor's intensity and speed of growth.

When we finally got to see Natalie, we noticed three incisions on her back, each about an inch long. Had the neurosurgeon cut her in three different places hoping to find a better sample? He was no longer around to ask. I remember thinking, *These are going to be the longest two days of our lives!*

The following forty-eight hours certainly felt like an eternity. Thankfully, numerous visitors stopped by the hospital, temporarily taking our minds off the situation. Having someone to sit with Natalie also allowed Tom and me to get out of the room for a while. Sometimes we just walked around the oncology floor, watching and praying over small children with little to no hair due to chemotherapy, many of them hooked to rolling IVs as they headed to and from various procedures. Seeing children in that condition broke my heart and made us wonder how parents who don't have a foundation of faith in a loving God could possibly handle situations like this.

*Where do they find their hope? I can't imagine burying my child in the ground if she doesn't make it, thinking that's the end and having to carry on for the rest of my life!*

The day after the biopsy was Valentine's Day. The waiting was difficult for all of us. But what struck me about that particular day was how Natalie strove to restore some normalcy to her life. She'd always enjoyed crafts and wanted to make Valentines for her classmates. A close friend brought over supplies, and Natalie carefully prepared a Valentine and printed a name for each classmate. On my way home to check on Will, I dropped the completed Valentines off at her school. As I did so, I prayed that Natalie's classmates would appreciate receiving the cards as much as Natalie had shown how much she valued all of them by taking time in her current state to write them each a card.

Later that evening, an adult friend who was battling cancer stopped by the hospital for a visit. While there, he told us about CaringBridge.org, a website that would allow us to send mass updates on Natalie's condition to family and friends. We were thankful for the suggestion. Grateful though we were that people cared, we already felt drained trying to process our own thoughts, much more so constantly repeating the same information to every person who checked in with us. That evening, Tom set up a site for Natalie. In the top banner, he posted our theme verse.

Trust in the LORD with all your heart and lean not on your own understanding; in all your ways submit to him, and he will make your paths straight. (Proverbs 3:5-6, NIV)

Throughout that week, I recited these verses over and over in my mind, even singing them mentally to a tune by which Will and Natalie had learned the Bible passage one summer during Vacation Bible School. Funny how things we don't even realize we retain emerge from our memory when we need them. The song brought comfort not only because of its meaning but also because of happy memories.

On Friday, February 15, our long wait for biopsy results was finally over. The morning dragged on, but around two o'clock, Tom and I were summoned for a meeting with the oncologist. The moment of truth was upon us, and I wasn't sure I was ready.

The meeting took place in a small room, which seemed to shrink even smaller with each moment we sat there. I am usually very detail-oriented, but all I remember is a table with two chairs on each side. The oncologist and the hospital's Family Life Specialist (FLS) assigned to Natalie's case sat on one side with Tom and me on the other. The rest was all a surreal blur. I felt as though I was having some out-of-body experience hovering up above everyone as I watched and listened in horror to the doctor's diagnosis.

"Natalie's spinal cord tumor is a malignant grade-three cancer. In fact, we actually believe it's a grade four. The neurosurgeon couldn't get a large enough sample to label it at the higher level without disturbing the tumor. But the medical protocols used for treatment will be the same regardless of whether it is grade three or four."

Tom and I listened with shock as there had been *no* indication right up to the last month. Who would have guessed a mild backache, tingly left leg and buttock, and constipation could be manifestations of such a deadly disease?

The oncologist went on to confirm that the tumor—known in clinical terms as an anaplastic astrocytoma—was the largest they'd ever seen and inoperable. In that moment, it felt like the air was sucked right out of the room as the doctor's words pierced deep into my heart. Our worst fears had been realized; our world as we knew it changed forever. Best case scenario, this would be a chronic illness for Natalie. Worst case, it could be terminal. Either case, our smart, happy, witty twelve-year-old was now facing the battle of her life.

And in a way, so were the rest of us. While Tom, Will, and I weren't fighting for our lives, we were now faced with a battle of our own. Would we lean into God or push him away?

# HELPS SECTION

## *Resources*

The news that a child or other loved-one is facing a life-threatening health crisis can be devastating for the family and leave them overwhelmed as to how to handle the situation. Thankfully, there are organizations and resources dedicated to helping families through such crises. Below are a few we can recommend that have been a great blessing to our family and others:

- **CaringBridge:** https://www.caringbridge.org/
- **Make-A-Wish:** https://wish.org/
- **Ronald McDonald House Charities:** https://www.rmhc.org/
- **American Cancer Society:** https://www.cancer.org/treatment /children-and-cancer/when-your-child-has-cancer.html
- **St Jude Children's Research Hospital:** https://www.stjude.org/
- **Cure Search for Children's Cancer:** https://curesearch.org/
- **St. Baldrick's Foundation:** https://www.stbaldricks.org/
- **American Brain Tumor Association:** https://www.abta.org/

6

# peace in
# the storm

"Anyone who listens to my teaching and follows it is wise,
like a person who builds a house on solid rock.
Though the rain comes in torrents and the floodwaters rise
and the winds beat against that house,
it won't collapse because it is built on bedrock."
—Matthew 7:24-25, NLT

Even though what I saw in that pediatric oncology conference room is still all a blur, Natalie's diagnosis was no surprise to me. I think deep down I'd already resolved in my mind the result would be cancer. I've always been inclined to lean toward the negative in my perspective of life's circumstances, more than anything as protection against hurt and disappointment.

"Better to be pleasantly surprised than disappointed," I've often told myself.

Thankfully, God knows and loves me, and he was already bringing to mind some of the many truths and promises he'd instilled in me over the past decade. Though what I'd feared the most as a mother had now come to pass, I wasn't feeling doubt or anger toward God. Rather, a single thought kept running through my mind. *I trust you, Lord. I trust you, Lord. I trust you, Lord.*

In fact, as I think back to that terrible day, I can see just how much God in his love and grace had done in my life to prepare me for this next, difficult leg of my faith journey. I love the ocean, as you may have guessed. As much now as an adult as when I was a child visiting the South Carolina shoreline on family vacations. Plop me down on any ocean beach, and the tension immediately drains from my body.

I'm overwhelmed by its sheer vastness and majesty and find myself immediately praising God for creating such a beautiful, complex body of water. I can sit for hours listening in total tranquility to the sound of surf crashing against the shore. The way the waves faithfully return no matter how much the land pushes them away is a reminder to me of God's loving, persistent pursuit during the years I chose to neglect him.

I'm just as mesmerized when a storm blows in. Lightning illuminates turbulent waters as they violently sweep everything in their path into the raging current. I marvel at the splendor yet tremble at the sheer power. It is majestic to watch from the protective safety of a stormproof shelter. But if I were caught out in that tempest, I would have little hope of survival.

Similarly, when the tumultuous waves came crashing down and swept me into the deep waters of my most painful trial, I could never have survived if God hadn't gone ahead of me, if he hadn't laid a bedrock foundation of unwavering trust in him beneath my feet. He was our family's sheltering wings, our refuge, and our safe place (Psalm 91) during the storm and in all the days since.

But my trust in God didn't suddenly emerge when Natalie became ill. Like the house built on solid rock in Matthew 7:24-25, my trust was built on years of opening my heart to God. Of honestly sharing my deepest hopes and fears, spending time in his Word, tuning my ear to his voice, and leaning into him—on the good days and the bad. I may have gotten off to a slow start, but just as the waves never abandon the shore, God never gave up on me. He ordered my steps and cultivated a bond of deep trust in him for an entire decade in anticipation of the storm to come.

I've mentioned the miracle by which God opened the door for me to start my own business, giving me the flexibility to participate fully in my children's school schedules and activities. Including the PTA (Parent-Teacher Association), where I served with a godly Christian woman who was battling a rare form of breast cancer. She passed away just a few months after I met her, leaving behind a husband and two young daughters. Her final words as she took her last breaths were a quote from scripture that expressed her absolute trust in God: "Walk by faith and not by sight" (2 Corinthians 5:7, KJV).

At the time, I struggled to understand how anyone could have experienced such deep peace and faith in God after enduring such a prolonged illness and knowing she was going to leave her family without a wife and mother. Would my own faith be strong enough to endure something so catastrophic? Wouldn't I feel angry and bitter? After several days of grappling with my emotions, God brought me to a place where I sincerely believed my faith could weather such a situation. But then my thoughts transitioned to my children.

*Okay, I believe I could handle dying and leaving my family,* I confessed to God. *But I'm not sure my faith is strong enough to sustain losing a child.*

At this time my children were thriving, so the likelihood of losing a child was inconceivable to me. I pushed the dark thought to the recesses of my mind and moved on with the day-to-day grind of life. But it was during this season that God began shaping me into a praying mother. The mothers' prayer group I'd joined at my church instilled in me the magnitude of my role as my children's advocate before God. I prayed daily for their relationships with God, friends, each other, Tom and me, their daily choices and actions, even their future spouses.

As I prayed, God helped me see that my children didn't belong to me and Tom but rather to him. He'd blessed us with the opportunity to be their parents, protectors, and greatest spiritual influence. Our responsibility was to teach them to love God, introduce them to Jesus, and do all we could to build a foundation of faith within our home, preparing them for the day when they would need to choose for themselves whether to follow God. God's grace in helping me grasp that my children were ultimately his and not ours would become a great comfort during my darkest days.

Around this time, I had the opportunity to attend a three-day spiritual retreat. The goal was to set aside all distractions and focus on God alone for a full seventy-two hours. That weekend, I experienced a pivotal moment while taking part in a special communion ceremony.

The directions were simple. Take a small piece of bread representing Christ's body broken for us (1 Corinthians 11:23-24), walk up to a large cross positioned at the front of the room, then place the piece of bread in a basket while verbally relinquishing anything standing between you and a life fully surrendered to Christ. As I waited my turn, I had it all planned out in my mind. *I'm going to ask God to help me stop feeling the need to be in control of everything in my life.*

As those ahead of me took their turn, I couldn't hear their words, but I could see by their visibly emotional body language that many were dealing with some pretty heavy stuff. Then it was my turn. I walked up front, stood in front of the cross, and was immediately overcome with emotion. I'd never experienced the presence of God so strongly, and I felt completely unworthy to be standing there. Opening my mouth to speak, I was totally taken aback by what came out. "Lord, help me surrender the fear of something happening to one of my children."

Laying my small piece of bread in the basket, I returned to my seat, tears pouring down my cheeks and in shock over what I'd just laid at the foot of the cross. Where in the world had that come from? I suddenly realized that the fear of losing a child that I'd considered and dismissed when my friend died of cancer was still festering within my subconscious.

As unsettling as this realization was, I felt a strange sense of peace that God had reached deep inside and pulled my fear into the light. I began praying for God's help and strength in surrendering this fear to him. And God answered. I'd been a worrier by nature all my life, even more so once I had children. Now God was teaching me to submit my children to his protective care through prayer. He also taught me that worry doesn't change the outcome but only reveals a lack of trust in his sovereignty. I mentioned earlier a project Natalie and I did together in writing out and memorizing Bible verses. Among the first verses I memorized were the apostle Paul's challenge to the Philippian church to stop worrying and experience God's peace instead.

> Don't worry about anything; instead, pray about everything. Tell God what you need, and thank him for all he has done. Then you will experience God's peace, which exceeds anything we can understand. His peace will guard your hearts and minds as you live in Christ Jesus. (Philippians 4:6-7, NLT)

The following summer, I participated in a life-changing Bible study called *Experiencing God* by Henry Blackaby. I learned a great deal from this study, including to "always view my circumstances against the backdrop of the cross, where God clearly demonstrated once and for all his deep love for me."[2]

Which brings me back to that terrible moment of listening to the details of Natalie's diagnosis in the pediatric oncology conference room. Despite overwhelming concern and pain, I could feel God's presence. I could hear his gentle reminder that this tsunami of a storm hadn't caught him by surprise. His tender voice whispered in my ear, *Never doubt my love for you. It was settled at the cross.*

I should have been terrified to see my worst fear realized. But long before this day, God had known what was coming and what I'd need to survive this storm. I've often heard that God uses life's storms to test what you know. Because I'd opened myself to spend the past decade learning about him, walking with him and filling my mind with his Word, his truth permeated my being. Because I'd made him my refuge and fortress in the wilderness, my house was built on a bedrock foundation no storm could sweep away. Instead of fear, anger, or bitterness, what I felt at that moment in that small, cramped, cold room was total trust and absolute peace. God's peace! And I knew that no matter what came next, I was going to be okay.

## HELPS SECTION
# *Tips for Visitors*

Visitors are a welcome reminder that people care and a distraction from a traumatic situation for the sick person as well as family. But entertaining a constant flood of visitors can also be draining. Here are a few tips to keep in mind when visiting a family or patient that is in a prolonged health crisis.

**During Hospital Stays:**

- **Call ahead rather than just show up.** Visitors were welcome, but it helped to know who, how many, and when. If Natalie was resting, we wanted her to be able to sleep. During her extended hospital stays, there was really only a short window during the day when she felt up to seeing people.

- **Offer to stay with the patient to give family members a break.** We always appreciated people who came to sit and chat with us, which was a nice distraction. But it was especially helpful when they volunteered to stay with Natalie so Tom and I could get out of the room for a while to take a shower, go for a walk, get something to eat, or just have some alone time to think and pray.

- **Bring favorite activities to help keep the patient's mind off the situation.** Many things visitors brought for Natalie were not readily available at the hospital, like her favorite snacks, crafts, books, or video games.

- **Consider a gift card instead of flowers or toys.** When Natalie was hospitalized for a month, the gas prices were very high. The cost of meals, drinks, and snacks for family members staying with a patient can add up quickly. A cash gift card can help with the expense of commuting back and forth from home to the hospital as well as other necessities. Gift cards for restaurants in or near the hospital or an offer to pick up a carry-out meal and bring it by is another way to bless the family.

**When At Home:**

- **Check the latest online update rather than calling or dropping by to ask** (e.g. CaringBridge, Facebook, or wherever updates are being posted). The family is typically exhausted, emotionally drained, and stretched for time. Not having to keep repeating the same update on the phone or in person is a big help.

- **Call to make sure a visit is welcome.** During hospital stays there is often little distraction beyond visiting. But once back home, the family may be too busy or stressed-out for drop-ins and the patient may also not be feeling up to visitors. It helped to know ahead when visitors were stopping by rather than having people just show up. We limited visitation during the timeframe of Natalie's chemo treatments as she felt especially sick then. This also reduced the risk of infection during those vulnerable periods.

# the new normal

"I look up to the mountains—does my help come
from there? My help comes from the LORD,
who made heaven and earth!"
—Psalm 121:1-2 (NLT)

I would need to cling to that peace and trust with all my strength because the following hours, days, and weeks proved a continuing nightmare. In less than a week, we'd gone from what we'd thought would be a basic visit to the pediatrician's office to a devastating diagnosis of cancer. How had this happened? What did we miss?

Among the oncologist's recommendations were immediate modifications to Natalie's diet, including the elimination of processed food, sugar, and any foods with nitrites—like hot dogs, pepperoni, and ham. *Sugar feeds cancer?* I was stunned to learn this. Sugar was Natalie's favorite food group. Tom routinely treated her to her favorite frozen cola drink while I often rewarded her with her favorite sour candy.

As for nitrites, I'd never heard the word before Natalie got sick. I cringed thinking of all the ham sandwiches, pepperoni pizza, and hot dogs we'd enjoyed together as a family. Not to mention all the pre-packaged lunches with their processed components I'd put in our children's lunchboxes over the years. Why had no one ever told us any of this? Had we contributed to our daughter's tumor?

Those questions still occasionally haunt me. Intellectually, I understood that eating these things didn't necessarily cause Natalie to develop a tumor. But emotionally, guilt still occasionally creeps in and consumes my thoughts if I don't immediately insert logic. *You didn't cause this, Kathy. Most kids have eaten these same foods, and they are fine. Will is fine.*

Sometime later when Tom had an appointment of his own with a neurologist, the doctor mentioned to him the possibility that there could have been something amiss with Natalie's astrocytes—neurological cells—as early as birth. I wish the doctor hadn't brought this up as Tom began wondering if the spinal tap Natalie had as a baby could have caused an abnormality resulting in the cancer. I offered the same counsel I'd given myself. "Lots of kids have had spinal taps, and they are fine."

But back then, sitting across from the oncologist as he laid out a proposed course of treatment, I couldn't let myself think such regrets. I needed to put on my best "strong mommy face" and focus on the task at hand, which was taking care of my little girl and doing all I could to help her beat this horrific disease. Whatever the options or outcomes, the trajectory of our lives was about to change drastically, and the prospect of what lay ahead was unsettling.

In my typical wish-for-the-best but brace-for-the-worst mentality, I still held onto the hope that God might grant Natalie a complete earthly healing. But I was also prepared for the possibility that he would heal her earthly body through death and give her a new eternal body in heaven. Obviously, I preferred the former. But my faith in Jesus Christ also gave me the assurance that, whatever happened, Natalie and I would be together one day in heaven.

Next came the hardest part. Tom and I had to tell our girl the bad news. Sharon, our Family Life Specialist, offered to go with us to explain the diagnosis. We took her up on her offer since a professional counselor might be helpful if Natalie had questions.

When the three of us entered her hospital room, Natalie was enjoying a number of visitors and appeared to be in a good mood. Flowers and scattered gifts softened the clinical austerity of the room. A whiteboard stood against one wall for visitors to scribble their "get-betters" and other well-wishes. The visitors got up to leave as soon as we asked to speak to Natalie alone. Most knew where we'd just been, and their expressions showed they understood only too well why we were clearing the room.

Sitting down on the bed beside Natalie, I took her hand in mine while Tom stood at the foot of the bed. Both of us were fighting back tears as Sharon explained to Natalie that she had cancer and outlined what the immediate future looked like in terms of treatment, including radiation and chemotherapy. It must have felt as unreal to our daughter as it did to us, and my heart almost shattered when she burst into tears.

A twelve-year-old girl's outward appearance is a large part of her identity, and the likelihood that she'd lose her hair seemed to distress Natalie as much as her actual illness. Thankfully, Sharon had comforting words to offer about the availability and high quality of wigs. This alleviated Natalie's fears—at least for the moment.

Needless to say, that Friday afternoon was a distressing time for the entire family. Will's baseball practice would be ending, so I headed home to be there when he walked in. Tears poured down my cheeks as I drove, and a knot twisted in my stomach as I considered how to tell Will that his only sibling had a potentially terminal disease. He knew, of course, that his sister had been in the hospital all week. And he knew some kind of mass had been found in her back. But with everything going on in his life between school and extracurricular activities, we'd decided not to get too detailed in explanations until we knew the final prognosis.

I made it in time to greet Will with a hug as he opened the door from our garage and walked into the kitchen. While I prepared dinner, I attempted to explain just how sick his sister was. Will had never been an outwardly emotional child, so I wasn't worried about an immediate explosion of sorrow and worry as much as what he might keep buried inside. I tried to paint an honest picture of what life might look like once Natalie returned home—though I myself really had no idea.

I also took the opportunity to share my heart about God's love for Natalie and our entire family. "Will, this diagnosis doesn't mean God loves us any less but that his plan for Natalie's life may be different than ours. We will walk this journey one day at a time, trusting God to carry us through."

Natalie was released from the hospital the next morning, Saturday, February 16. Since Will didn't have school, he chose to come to the hospital with me so we could all return home as a family. As the doctor signed her release papers, he explained that Natalie would start her treatment over the next few weeks. But the first step would be surgery to install a port-a-catheter, a flexible tube inserted into a major vein just under the skin through which IV (intravenous) drips, medications, and chemotherapy could be injected without constant needle pricks.

As Tom, Will, and I wheeled Natalie downstairs and rolled onto the sidewalk outside the hospital, it struck me how real it was starting to feel. We would now be on our own at home without round-the-clock hospital staff, trying to figure out how best to keep Natalie comfortable and healthy. These thoughts were whirling through my mind on the drive home when Natalie's sweet little voice suddenly broke into my reflections from the back seat. "So can I get a cell phone now?"

She'd asked for a phone at the beginning of the school year. We'd told her she'd have to wait till eighth grade like her brother. Turning around in the front passenger seat, I gave Natalie my "we've talked about this" look. She responded with a sly smile. "Well, how am I going to call you guys from school if something goes wrong or I'm not feeling well?"

*She has a point!* I remember thinking, *That girl has certainly figured out how to get what she wants!*

Tom and I agreed to take Natalie shopping for a phone before she started back to school. Thankfully, her oncologist had approved her return to classes once the IV drip was administered to build up her immune system. I shared the incident with a friend a few days later, and he sent Natalie a brand-new flip phone that same week. Of course, she ended up using the phone for more than reporting on her health status. Including texting Tom on occasion to bring her some favorite food item if she didn't like what he'd packed her for lunch. And Tom would bring it, unable to resist a plea from his little girl.

Once Natalie got past the initial shock and fear, our little girl kicked into survivor mode, focusing her energy on fighting the cancer while living her life in the best way possible. One of the first things she requested after her diagnosis was a new photo album such as we'd created together years earlier to hold index cards with verses we'd chosen to memorize. With her new cell phone, she started texting friends and family members, asking them to send her their favorite Bible verses. She wrote these out on her index cards and placed them in the new album, which she'd decorated.

She quoted these verses for strength and inspiration throughout her ordeal. Her chosen life verse had always been, "For I can do everything through Christ, who gives me strength" (Philippians 4:13, NLT). But she soon started quoting another verse almost as regularly: "For nothing will be impossible with God" (Luke 1:37, ESV).

She needed that strength and encouragement as the following weeks would have been physically and mentally grueling for anyone, even more so for a preadolescent twelve-year-old. On February 26, less than two weeks after being told her cancer was malignant, she started six weeks of radiation every morning Monday through Friday. When we arrived at the clinic for her first treatment, the nurse escorted her back to a dressing room to put on a gown while Tom and I were escorted to the radiologist's office.

"How long do you think the tumor has been there?" I asked him, a question to which we hadn't yet been able to get a clear answer.

"Based on its size and spread, I'd estimate twelve to eighteen months," he responded.

Tom and I just stared at him with our mouths agape. How was it possible such a horrible, huge, deadly mass had been growing inside our daughter for such a long time without any of us having a clue, including her pediatrician? How different might the situation be now if we'd known all this a year ago?

I will always wonder if there were earlier signs of trouble we should have noticed. But it was too late now to be second-guessing might-have-beens. The radiologist went over the procedure and potential side effects. Then we joined Natalie in the room where the radiation machine was housed. The technician had "mapped" where she would receive the radiation, which showed up as three green Xs aligned across the middle of her back. Running up her spine just above the Xs were the three perpendicular scars from her biopsy incisions, still looking red and raw. The treatment itself only took about ten minutes. Then Natalie was off to school. The very normality of it all seemed bizarre.

For the next month Monday through Friday, Tom took Natalie to the radiologist each morning at seven o'clock. By eight-thirty, she would be at school. Between the radiation and chemo, the side effects were slight nausea, headaches, and fatigue. But she courageously pushed through these, most days making it through lunch before she had to call and ask Tom to bring her home. We were a little nervous about her being exposed to germs at school, but we also knew continued routine was important to her emotional health. She was receiving an antibiotic to help with her immune system, so we had to trust God to keep her safe from infection.

## HELPS SECTION

# *Breaking the News*

Before communicating the traumatic information of a life-threatening diagnosis, you will want to think through how best to break the news, especially if the patient is a young child or even a teenager. When informed of Natalie's diagnosis, we were asked if we wanted to tell her or if we preferred the hospital's Family Life Specialist (FLS) to do it. Feeling ill-equipped for the task, we opted for the FLS with us present. There is no right way, but here are some points to consider from our own experience.

- **Be honest when answering their questions.** Natalie asked a lot of questions, so we needed to be ready with answers. The medical staff can help with what to say and prepare you for questions that may be raised. And if you can't find an answer, it's okay to say that you don't know but will try to find out.

- **Don't try to hide or minimize the severity of their condition.** We may think we're protecting our loved-one by avoiding their questions or misrepresenting the truth, but they know their bodies better than we ever can, and older kids especially will realize when something feels different or not right. They may stop asking us and start asking others if they feel we are hiding something.

- **Be as honest as possible about your own feelings.** You don't need to express your fear that they are going to die. But it may help them open up more if you confess that you too are scared, worried, and sad about their illness.

- **Speak positively about the health-care professionals.** This builds confidence in the medical personnel caring for them when your loved-one sees that you trust them.

- **Involve them in treatment decisions (if age appropriate).** Natalie wanted to understand the purposes of medicines and treatments. She wanted to know what to expect from each treatment, and her doctor tried to explain in a manner that she could grasp.

8

# the ones
# who walk with us

"Don't look out only for your own interests,
but take an interest in others, too."
—Philippians 2:4 (NLT)

One blessing in this nightmare was that Tom had still been working part-time from home when Natalie was diagnosed. We were
deeply thankful for how God had worked out the timing so he could be
her primary caregiver while I was at work. Tom displayed a gift for handling Natalie's medical issues so comfortably and competently it made
me wonder if he'd missed a career calling in health care.

The tingling in Natalie's left buttock and leg that had led to her
diagnosis had now degenerated into a limp that inhibited her mobility,
especially with a book bag. So Tom began driving to the middle school
throughout the school day to walk her from one class to the next as well
as bringing her lunches that fit the food modifications the oncologist had
stipulated.

Natalie's principal, staff, and teachers were also supportive in every
way. They understood that she had radiation prior to starting her school
day so would likely need to go home and rest by early afternoon. Her last
class before lunch was language arts, and the teacher allowed her to stay

there to eat the lunch Tom had prepared for her rather than having to limp to the cafeteria. She'd started playing flute the year before, and her band instructor arranged to have an extra flute at school so she didn't have to carry hers.

As was typical for Natalie, she refused to use her illness as a crutch for opting out or offering less than her best. Like any twelve-year-old, she might gripe occasionally about the drudgery of homework, but she completed all her assignments on time. From the beginning, her school friends helped her when she needed assistance, and Giovanna especially always stuck close whenever Natalie was there.

Even so, I don't think we'd have made it through this journey without the many others who lovingly and caringly gave of their own time and resources to walk with us. I'm normally a very independent person. I don't ask for help unless I'm in dire straits. Maybe this stems from pride, wanting people to believe I can manage it all by myself. Maybe it's because I'm a middle child who developed an independent streak. Maybe I'm just afraid to relinquish control of what's happening around me.

I doubt I'll ever really understand my desire for self-sufficiency. But it didn't take me long to recognize that managing a catastrophic illness while trying to maintain some sense of normalcy in our home was beyond my capacity. It had all happened so quickly that it felt like we were flung into the deep end of a pool with weights tied to our feet. The mere thought of handling routine tasks like running errands, housecleaning, and cooking coupled with everything that now needed to happen to care for Natalie seemed insurmountable. We knew we might quickly drown without the help of others to push us back to the surface of that deep end for air.

Thankfully, our close friends, family, and countless others, including a number of people we'd never met, came to our rescue. For the entirety of Natalie's illness, we felt extremely loved and well-cared-for. It was a huge relief to know we had people ready to provide assistance in every way possible. We only needed to ask once, and it was done. If friends and family felt helpless to take away our pain, they tried all the harder to help alleviate our stress in those tangible ways that they could. With such a strong support system in place, we knew we weren't going to have to walk this dark and terrifying path alone.

This included meals different friends, family, and work colleagues prepared for us each week. Some people ran errands while others brought activities for Natalie to help keep her mind off her illness. Whether during Natalie's hospital stays or at home, people would volunteer to stay with Natalie so Tom and I could have some away time, be it together or alone. My leadership at work was sympathetic and accommodating, allowing me the flexibility to come in late, leave early, and be at every doctor appointment.

We were also humbled by the number of people who reached out to let us know they were thinking about us. Just to know that people were praying was calming. Receiving an encouraging note or text—especially when no return response was expected—meant so much on those days when we felt like circumstances were just too much to bear.

When dealing with a chronically sick child, simply providing distractions to make them feel like a normal kid, if just for a little while, is a big blessing. Friends took Natalie on walks in her wheelchair. They brought crafts when they visited and worked on them with her. A friend arranged Carrie Underwood concert tickets and got a softball bat autographed for her. My work colleagues raised money to buy her a golf cart so she could get out of the house and ride around the neighborhood. All these things helped take her mind off of doctor visits, hospitals, and tests.

One major difficulty of dealing with one child's health crisis is ensuring that any other children in the household don't feel neglected when Mom and Dad's focus always seems to be on the sick sibling. We did our best to make sure at least one of us was there for Will when he came home from school or had ball games and other activities, especially during times when Natalie was in the hospital. But we were also thankful for family and friends who planned special activities or gifts for Will so he wouldn't feel left out.

One such blessing was a used car my parents bought Will for his sixteenth birthday because they wanted him to feel special on his big day.

This also checked a box on our "to do" list as we didn't have time to car shop or find transportation to and from school and baseball for him. Recently, Will and I were chatting about this time period, and I asked him if he ever felt resentful or neglected during Nat's illness.

"No, I never did," he responded immediately. "You and Dad allowed me to live as normally as possible. My daily activities didn't change. If I'd had to quit playing baseball or been stressed out from having to balance my schoolwork with extra responsibilities taking care of my sister, I might have felt resentful. But thanks to you and Dad, my life was able to continue as usual, and other than being really concerned that Nat was sick, nothing seemed different."

It was a very precious affirmation that *both* of our children felt loved and cared for at this critical time in their lives.

On the other hand, not everything people did in an attempt to be helpful was beneficial, although we knew people had good intentions. Let me share just a few of those, not to complain, but simply as helpful examples if you might be dealing with a similar situation.

First, pat spiritual phrases like "God is in control" or "everything happens for a reason" were not comforting. We were quite well aware in our heads of the correct theology, but at this moment we were wrapped up in our hearts. Our child was hurting, and we just wanted to make it stop.

Also not helpful was when people felt compelled to share their own stories of similar situations, including medical testing and results. I've been guilty of this myself, so I understand their motive was to encourage us. But it didn't accomplish the intended goal. In truth, if they told us how their child had gone through a similar diagnosis and everything turned out okay, it just fostered false hope. If their child's results weren't good and there was no happy ending, it just discouraged us further, intensifying our anxiety each time we awaited test results.

Thankfully, Natalie with her usual aplomb just let such unhelpful talk roll off her like water from a well-oiled surface. She was discerning when it came to the interpersonal areas of her life, and I realize now that her mental depth and capacity helped her grasp the magnitude of her situation. She asked a lot of questions at her weekly checkups when the doctor reviewed her bloodwork results. She was curious about her white blood cell counts because she quickly picked up on what levels might require a transfusion.

Ironically, Natalie's first major hurdle wasn't the side effects from the radiation treatments but figuring out how to swallow her oral chemotherapy drug, which she started just two days after beginning radiation. She'd always struggled with taking medications in pill form, so we'd typically given her liquid pain relievers and antibiotics. I will never forget how annoyed she was when we opened the prescription package to discover a container full of pills. Then we read the directions: "Take 105 milligrams per day by mouth." One pill was a hundred milligrams while a second one contained five milligrams.

"Seriously?" she exclaimed. "They couldn't just stuff the extra five milligrams into the other pill?!"

I didn't blame her. It was bad enough she had to master taking oral meds. Now it was two pills each day—with such a ridiculously small dosage in the second pill! Maybe her heavenly Father just wanted to teach Natalie to trust his power to overcome these challenges from the get-go.

When we gave Natalie the first pill on March 1, she struggled to get it down. Over and over, she tried washing it down with water, but she just couldn't get it far enough back in her throat. She finally burst into tears. "I can't do it!"

I started to panic since we'd been told these pills shouldn't dissolve in her mouth but in her stomach. I had no idea what to do if she wasn't successful in getting it down. At a complete loss for any other solution, I began to pray. At what felt like the absolute last moment before the pill dissolved on Natalie's tongue, she pushed it as far back as she could and once again swallowed. This time it went down. God had provided. One down, one to go.

But facing another pill was more than Natalie could take. She started to cry again. "I can't do this for forty-one more days!"

"God has just shown you that he is with you and will help you," I assured her gently.

Sure enough, the second pill proved easier to swallow than the first. Within a few days, she was popping those pills into her mouth and swallowing them like a pro. She credited prayer for her newfound ability to swallow them.

"The prayer and support are awesome and pull me through!" she wrote on CaringBridge. "I can always count on y'all … Every night before pill time, I always pray and can go online and read all of your comments. It makes me feel so good, and I say, 'I can do it!' It touches me and makes me stronger to know how many people are there for me."

Due to swelling around the tumor, Natalie was placed on a regular steroid regimen. This reduced the swelling but created severe stretch marks on her body. These were raw and painful when they first appeared but then became another visible representation that her body didn't look the way she wanted. Natalie asked me, "When I'm better, could we get something to make them go away?"

I tried to assure her most people wouldn't notice while promising we'd make every attempt to get rid of them. I had no idea what that might be. I figured we'd cross that bridge when the time came. But these conversations always had me in tears the minute I left her presence because I know how hard it is to be an adolescent girl with body image issues. I tried to focus on the positive aspect of our conversation—the fact that she was still hopeful of being healed.

Outside of school, Natalie's weeks were filled with doctor's appointments, radiation treatments, and chemo infusions. We were always relieved when her blood cell counts were good and no transfusion was necessary. The chemo infusions began after the first round of oral chemo and were far more brutal in their extreme side effects. Natalie dreaded these days because she knew it meant an extra level of nausea, fatigue, and loss of appetite. But she seldom whined. I recall only a few times when she just didn't have it in her to go. She was tired of feeling awful with no tangible results. I understood. I didn't want to go either, and I wasn't the one with poison infusing my body.

But most days she'd put on her game face and roll into the clinic where she'd greet the staff cordially, sometimes even joking with them. Then she'd sit for hours while the drugs entered her body. Once home, she'd rest, pushing through the side effects while focusing on the end goal of winning the raging battle the chemo was fighting inside her. She gave a whole new meaning to the old adage, "The end justifies the means."

Gone was the little girl who rang the bell incessantly over the smallest discomfort or inconvenience. Natalie was now a strong young lady who immensely disliked her current state but consistently thanked us and her health-care providers for caring for her.

## HELPS SECTION

# *Providing a Support System*

Friends, extended family, church members, colleagues, and others often want to help during an ongoing crisis but don't know how or what offers of assistance would be most helpful. Here are some ways in which we were blessed with practical aid that most families in crisis would appreciate.

- **Offer assistance with day-to-day tasks.** This may include running errands such as picking up items from the grocery store or drug store, general maintenance, and child care.

- **Prepare and deliver meals on a regular basis.** Meals that can be frozen and reheated later are especially helpful in case unexpected hospital visits arise. One friend offered to coordinate a meal schedule. We were able to direct everyone from our support system to her so she could handle the scheduling details.

- **Volunteer to maintain the yard.**

- **Offer to clean the house.** Keeping a clean house was important due to Natalie's illness, but many days we just couldn't get to it.

- **Volunteer as on-call chauffeur.** One friend took Tom to a doctor's appointment when he needed someone to stay with him and I couldn't leave Natalie. Other children of the family may also need transportation assistance to school or church activities.

- **Be considerate and flexible if you are the employer or supervisor of someone going through such a family crisis.** Offer flexible schedules that permit coming in late, leaving early, and being at doctor appointments.

Any help is appreciated, but the timing of the need(s) may vary. Asking will help ensure you meet the most immediate need. Many resource websites allow the family to create a schedule of tasks, communicating exactly what is needed and enlisting willing volunteers so the family doesn't feel overwhelmed.

9

# in the trenches

"Are any of you sick? You should call for the elders of the
church to come and pray over you, anointing you with oil in
the name of the Lord. Such a prayer offered in faith will
heal the sick, and the Lord will make you well."
— James 5:14–15 (NLT)

On March 16, our church held a healing service where our pastor, family, and friends gathered to pray, sing, and anoint Natalie with oil as instructed in the New Testament epistle of James. During the service, we were introduced to the beautiful song by Christian contemporary music artist Natalie Grant, "In Better Hands." The lyrics speak of the hope of being cradled in God's loving "better hands" when faith runs out and trials come. The song really touched Natalie, and she later did an illustrated drawing of what the song meant to her.

Spring break rolled around in April, and we took a much-needed beach vacation with extended family. Like me, Natalie always loved the ocean. This trip was special because her closest cousin, my older sister's daughter, Bailey, was there. The two cousins were just ten days apart in age and had always been "thick as thieves." At extended family gatherings, we rarely saw one without the other standing next to her. Beach trips with family were something we did every summer, so this felt somewhat close to normal life for all of us.

Natalie struggled with her limp but was still feeling well enough to enjoy the sand and waves. We weren't as diligent with the sunblock as we should have been, adding sunburned legs to her list of ailments. But overall the trip was a nice distraction, and it took our minds off Natalie's upcoming MRI, scheduled for April 25.

The MRI results weren't what we'd hoped for, although they could have been much worse. Though the tumor wasn't growing, it wasn't shrinking either. I wanted to be grateful—and I was to some degree. But I was also intensely disappointed because I'd allowed myself to believe the chemo might kill the tumor. The doctors consulting on Natalie's case decided to try a different regimen of chemotherapy drugs, hoping this one might actually shrink the tumor.

Undeterred by the results, Natalie decided to do something special for Will's sixteenth birthday. Since Will loves chocolate, she baked a pan-sized brownie and handcrafted a card to go with it. I found the card again recently. Here is what she wrote inside.

Happy 16th birthday! Hope you have an awesome birthday! You are the greatest brother in the world, and you deserve the best birthday ever! Thanks for everything you do. I really appreciate it. If you ever need anything, let me know and I'll try my best … Blow out the candles and make a great big wish … Love you bunches and bunches, Shorty. XOXOXOXO

We celebrated Mother's Day on Sunday, May 11. Will and Natalie had each made me a card and presented me with a huge balloon. After the morning worship service, Tom and the kids took me out for lunch. It almost felt like any other Mother's Day—other than the impending dread we were all feeling over the new round of chemotherapy, which would start the next day.

We drove the next morning to the clinic, where two drugs were administered intravenously through Natalie's port-a-catheter. It was a long, boring day since it took almost eight hours of sitting while the drugs slowly entered her body. By the time we got home, we were all exhausted. But Natalie also felt nauseated and just wanted to crash. We got her into bed, where she fell asleep.

The next morning when Natalie woke up, her back was hurting badly and her legs wouldn't hold her weight, so much that Tom had to carry her to the bathroom. Tom and I tried not to panic so Natalie wouldn't be as alarmed. We called her doctor, who suspected the swelling in her spine was compressing the affected nerves. He increased her steroid dosage to help reduce the swelling and scheduled another MRI for later in the week. He also arranged a wheelchair for her to use while he researched the possibilities of regaining strength in her legs.

Now Natalie wasn't just an adolescent with cancer but one who could no longer walk. She, of course, had no idea what had just happened over-night to her already broken body, and it was heartbreaking to witness her fear.

"Please, God!" I pleaded in prayer. "No more!"

To pile onto this mountain of calamity, the new MRI showed that the damage to Natalie's legs was likely irreversible. Any hope of our little girl returning to a normal life was diminishing with each passing day. I still couldn't wrap my head around how quickly things had gotten this bad. I'd even allowed myself to be somewhat optimistic about a full recovery. But now for the first time the strong possibility began to settle in my mind that she wasn't going to make it. The tumor just seemed unstoppable.

I know Tom was as scared as I was that we were going to lose her. But he never let on with Natalie. He was a steadfast rock in caring for her during this period—calm, positive, attentive, gentle, and loving. I stood in awe watching him clean and access her port-a-catheter with the medicines she needed. He slept in her room to be available if she needed anything during the night. Like most fathers, he adored his little girl and wanted to protect her from harm. His heart ached that she was so sick and that he was powerless to fix it. Taking care of her made him feel he was doing all he humanly could to help with her healing and make her life as comfortable as possible.

Natalie expressed her appreciation in her journal. "Nurse Dad is pretty good if I do say so myself. Actually great. He learned quickly and does it very well."

But Natalie was still a normal twelve-year-old girl. Tom didn't give in to her every demand just because she was sick. If she felt he wasn't appropriately coddling her, she was quick to call me at work or tell me when I got home. I think more than anything she was just bored and wanted to call me. They battled occasionally over small things like Tom's choice of meals. But overall they formed a solid team that made a horrible situation bearable for our family because they didn't focus on the minor setbacks of the day. They'd typically share with Will and me only the bigger health issues or lighten the mood by recounting funny situations that popped up amidst their daily routine.

One unpleasant side effect of the steroids was water retention and weight gain. Within a very short period, Natalie gained over thirty pounds. Her inability to walk coupled with the reality that she now weighed as much as I did meant Tom was the only one able to carry her. We again saw how God had gone ahead of us in preparing our family life so that Tom was the one home during the day instead of me.

Natalie's middle school continued to be accommodating. Her assignments were sent home so she could complete them in a more comfortable environment. The school excused her from the end-of-grade standardized testing, but Natalie wanted to finish strong. On May 21, I rolled her into school in her wheelchair, and she took her end-of-grade math test. She was exhausted but felt a sense of accomplishment.

The next day, she returned and pushed through the remaining tests. She gave it her best effort, and we were proud when the principal called to tell us she'd achieved high scores. Even in the midst of side effects from radiation and chemotherapy, she finished the school year as an honor student. She attended the end-of-year awards ceremony because she wanted to say goodbye to everyone for the summer. She believed she'd be back in the fall for the start of her seventh-grade year, and we were hopeful she would as well.

Natalie's drive to live a normal life was as unstoppable as her cancer. Even after she became bedridden, she wanted to use her time constructively. She asked my sister-in-law, Sheila, herself a breast cancer survivor, to help her make bracelets she could sell to raise needed funds for our church's youth group. She called these "Beadattitudes" and ended up selling enough to donate several hundred dollars. For each bracelet she created a card that read, "My purpose in making and selling these bracelets is to glorify God."

My birthday was in late May, and Tom and I decided to get away for some time together. We knew we were leaving Natalie in good hands with my parents and my sister. Still, neither of us felt comfortable venturing too far so we stayed in a local hotel. Natalie texted us the whole weekend. It was hard to keep the right perspective and not get upset, especially since her pattern for years had been to try and make us feel guilty anytime we left her and Will for a date night.

In hindsight, I know having us around brought Natalie a sense of comfort because we'd know what to do if anything went wrong. And considering what she'd experienced over the past four months, she had every reason to worry that something could go wrong. In the end, we decided to return home earlier than planned just for her sense of security.

And I'm glad we did as that was my last birthday I'd get to spend with my daughter. She made me the sweetest birthday card. We spent the rest of the day sitting on her bed playing board games, watching movies, and drawing.

By early June, Natalie had developed a huge pressure ulcer—or bedsore—on her bottom. The pain was excruciating, and as much as we rotated her position in the bed, the sore would not heal. A numbing cream was prescribed, but it proved totally ineffective. After almost a month, the doctor finally hospitalized her to prevent the sore from abscessing. The nurses applied a protective paste to the affected area, which offered some relief. They also started giving her anesthesia during her MRIs as the bedsore made it difficult for her to lie still for two-and-a-half hours each time. The bedsore continued to plague her throughout the summer and disrupted her ability to enjoy activities that required sitting for pro-longed periods of time.

Natalie's oncologist was on the board of the local Make-A-Wish chapter. Soon after her diagnosis, he let us know that she qualified for a special wish. She chose a family trip for all four of us to a popular international waterpark, which was scheduled for early July.

Looking back, we should have realized this wasn't the best idea since the trip involved a lot of sitting. But our brains were so fatigued we didn't think through the implications, and after all the hard work the charity's staff had put into the trip, we hated to cancel. With the endless doctor appointments and continuing health issues, we just wanted our girl to have a fun break from what life had become and do something she'd always wanted to do.

But the trip ended up being a miserable experience for her. The pain from her pressure ulcer was off the charts, and she'd lost her ability to control her bowel functions, which made venturing far from our hotel room a major challenge. One day, we decided to take Natalie for a ride down the resort's lazy river. The young ride attendant watched while Tom, Will, and I painstakingly loaded Natalie into an inner tube, climbed into our own, and floated out into the current. Only then did he bother to inform us that the ride was being shut down due to weather.

We were now on the opposite side of the river from where we'd left the wheelchair. We asked the attendant if he could help us push Natalie back against the current so we could lift her out on that side. It was quickly apparent we would receive no assistance from the employee, so we pulled Natalie out of the tube where the current had carried us. Tom sent Will to get the wheelchair, but he had to go around the full perimeter of the park to retrieve it and was gone for quite a while.

In the meantime, Tom carried Natalie over to a lounge chair. With her weight and the slipperiness of her limp, wet body, he almost dropped her several times, and I'm sure she could feel his sense of panic. When we finally reached the chair, she began to sob, "I just want to go home! I just want to go home!"

Tom and I felt responsible for her distress since we should have known better than to attempt this trip in her condition. Thankfully, the Make-A-Wish team had arranged a very special visit for Natalie with the resort's trained dolphins to finish off her trip. This proved a very positive experience, and her spirits perked up. The dolphin training staff worked with her deficiencies and made her feel special.

Though the trip was not a complete success due to our own lack of foresight, we are so grateful to the Make-a-Wish Foundation for their generosity. All the work they put into the trip was amazing, and though none of our troubles were their fault, they graciously gave Natalie a brand-new laptop to make up for the difficulties she'd experienced.

In late July, Natalie started physical therapy. The hospital fitted her for leg braces. These extended to her hips and were supposed to allow her to lock her knees and hips while stretching or strengthening her leg muscles. We'd hoped they would also allow her to have a break from sitting or lying in bed, which should help with the bed sores. Natalie's spirits were the lowest I'd seen them, and I really hoped this would encourage her. She texted me at work on July 24: "Please pray for a miracle that God will allow me to walk again."

I cried as I read the text, then prayed for a miracle as she'd asked. It took her being in heaven for my prayer to be answered. But our sweet girl is indeed walking, skipping, and jumping again.

Natalie had dreams for her future. She was looking forward to the rest of her life. In an elementary school assignment, she'd outlined her short-term goals for middle school and high school and her long-term goals for college and career. Like most girls her age, her list included items like making friends, getting good grades, playing sports, and participating in organized activities. But she'd also listed character goals:

- Don't let anyone try to pull me down the wrong path.
- Stand up for what is right even if I stand alone.
- Be a leader and role model.

She had aspirations of getting into a college with a good medical school. Once there, she listed her goals as:

- Study hard.
- Do well in college and get all my work done.
- Become a pediatrician and be excellent at my career.

Now my sweet, smart, caring, ambitious girl's daily life consisted of a raw bottom and waking up every hour because she couldn't get comfortable. Her bowel issues progressed from constipation to diarrhea. Her stomach felt tight, and she was starting to experience headaches, which was new. Tom was exhausted from being up with her all night. We finally decided to contract overnight care to ensure her comfort.

When school started in August, there was no question of Natalie returning to regular classes. The school system provided a teacher a few times a week who worked with her on English, math, social studies, and science. She was really trying to keep her chin up, but it seemed to her that everything was going wrong and getting worse.

"Can't I quit this chemo?" she finally begged me. "It makes me feel *so* bad!"

I couldn't disagree with her since she did seem to be feeling worse by the day. We weren't sure if it was the buildup of toxins in her system, but she was having more and more bouts with nausea and increasing trouble keeping food down. We felt so helpless!

But though the chemo drained her, Natalie still conjured up enough energy to insist on getting out of the house. She wanted to go out to lunch, to dinner, or to the mall. Getting out was good for her spirits, and we actually heard her sweet laugh for the first time in a long while. Our biggest goal by this point was just to bring our little girl some joy. We were grateful to God for every small victory.

HELPS SECTION

## *A New Normal*

A terminally ill family member in the home completely changes daily life and routine. Here are just a few hard-learned tips we wish someone had told us at the outset.

- **Be flexible.** Your schedule or routine can change immediately. Every time we thought our lives were in a consistent pattern, Natalie would experience an unanticipated issue. Because an illness can come with so many unknowns, be ready to drop everything and handle the issue.

- **Always have overnight bags packed.** Not just for the sick family member but also for whoever may need to stay overnight with the patient in the hospital.

- **Keep the family situation as normal as possible.** Try to maintain typical routines (e.g. meal times, bed times, etc.).

- **Ask for a flexible work schedule**. Most employers are willing to work with you in an ongoing crisis so that as needed you can come in late, leave early, and be at doctor appointments. If your particular supervisor or workplace is unwilling, you may need to talk to the human resource department or even a lawyer about your legal options.

- **Don't allow your fears to keep them in a bubble.** We were concerned Natalie's immune system might not handle public outings, but we quickly realized her emotional health was better for it.

- **Be prepared for the side effects of treatment.** This includes asking your health-care providers what to expect and what supplies you may need to keep your loved-one comfortable. Natalie never experienced the typical side effect of chemo we expected—hair loss. But we weren't prepared for the extreme weight gain and stretch marks caused by the steroids. Had I been forewarned, perhaps I could have applied some form of cream to help prevent the severity.

- **Prepare your ill loved-one for their interactions with others.** This includes not just family and friends but strangers as well. Natalie was in a wheelchair and quite swollen so people often stared. Some even went so far as to make rude comments out of ignorance. Over time, we were better equipped to respond and to help Natalie understand and ignore inconsiderate behavior. For close personal friends, it may help to let your loved-one take the first step in reaching out, demonstrating to the friend a desire to maintain the relationship.

- **If your ill loved-one is school-age, keep an open line of communication with the school.** Natalie's treatment interfered with school work and attendance. We asked her doctor to outline her medical condition and limitations in writing to give to the school administration. We also kept an open line of communication with Natalie's teachers as to what work needed to be made up as well as any necessary adjustments to help her during the school day.

10

# joy in
# the moment

"Answer me when I call to you, my righteous God.
Give me relief from my distress;
have mercy on me and hear my prayer."
—Psalm 4:1 (NIV)

"Mom, why do you think God isn't answering our prayers for healing?" Natalie asked me one morning.

Her question caught me off guard. I knew that in God's sovereign design death is our ultimate healing, and I understood that our prayers for Natalie's healing might be answered in that manner. But such blunt honesty wasn't what my daughter needed at that moment. She'd maintained such a hopeful disposition thus far, and I didn't want to dampen her spirits. So I set aside my typical directness and offered a realistic but softened and tender response.

"I don't know for sure, honey. God hears all our prayers, but he doesn't always answer in our desired timeframe or in ways we expect or want. We will never really understand his purpose until we stand in God's presence and he shows us. For all we know, God may be answering my prayer that you wouldn't succumb to peer pressure. It's hard for you to be doing things you shouldn't be as long as you are here and not out with friends."

This wasn't the first time Natalie had asked a deep spiritual question as she tried to understand how God might be working through her illness. Our spiritual conversations over the years had been meaningful moments for me, and I realized now how profoundly they'd impacted my daughter as well. When I came home from work, I'd often find her sitting up in her bed, reading the Bible passages she'd written out and placed in her new photo album. During her lengthiest hospital stay in September 2008, she did drawings to illustrate some of these scriptures. She hadn't brought her photo album to the hospital, so she'd clearly memorized them. In her darkest moments, she was claiming God's promises and finding comfort in God's Word.

I used her current question about why God wasn't answering our prayers as a transition to bring up the comfort God had provided in the Old Testament book of Psalms. "God knows what you're feeling, and he wants you to be honest and open in expressing your emotions to him. That's why he gave us the book of Psalms, which is packed full of God's children expressing pretty much every emotion there is."

I showed her some examples. Joy in Psalm 95. Sadness and discouragement in Psalm 43. Fear in Psalm 27. Anger in Psalm 44. Hopelessness in Psalm 77. Crying out for mercy in Psalm 28.

"Do you see, honey, how God is showing us through these psalms that we are never alone? It doesn't matter how desperate we become or what our emotions are when we cry out to him. We can still put our hope in him because he will never leave us."

Natalie nodded her understanding, then asked, "Can we start reading a psalm each day?"

I leaned in for a hug. "Absolutely!"

From then on, Tom and I took turns reading the Psalms with her. She also committed some of the passages to memory and illustrated a few of her favorites to include in her photo album:

Lord, you are my shield, my wonderful God who gives me courage. (Psalm 3:3, NCV)

Answer me when I pray to you, my God who does what is right. Make things easier for me when I am in trouble. (Psalm 4:1, NCV)

I have set the Lord always before me; because he is at my right hand, I will not be shaken. (Psalm 16:8, ESV).

Thy word is a lamp unto my feet, and a light unto my path. (Psalm 119:105, KJV)

I wait for the Lord to help me, and I trust his word. (Psalm 130:5, NCV)

Focusing on these psalms reminded us as Natalie's parents and as a family of God's unwavering love and concern. It kept our own outlook hopeful and encouraged a spirit of gratitude within us. Over half the scripture verses Natalie illustrated were from the Psalms, so I knew she was reflecting on those verses regularly and used them to share what was deep within her heart.

Natalie also used her online journal, text exchanges, and artwork to express herself during this difficult time. Jessie, a college-age friend we knew from Will's school who'd lost her mother to cancer, became her pen pal. Writing letters back and forth with Jessie was a continuous source of comfort and support throughout her ordeal.

But Natalie wasn't one to dwell on her feelings. I've heard since of similar responses in others going through life-threatening trials. Maybe they just accepted the situation or didn't want their loved-ones to see how scared they really were. For Natalie, it might have been a defense mechanism to keep her mind in a better place since negativity can beget negativity.

It wasn't that Natalie denied that she felt bad or pretended things were better than they were. She was always transparent. She simply chose to tell people how she was feeling, solicit prayer cover, then focus her energy on improving her situation rather than assuming it would stay the same or worsen. Four months into her cancer battle, as her sixth-grade school year drew to a close, Natalie wrote the following about her summer plans.

Even if I can't do everything I wanted to this summer quite as easily, we can find stuff to do to make it fun, wheelchair or not. It's still not the simplest thing, but I'm pretty used to it now, and sometimes it's nice to catch a free ride around places anyhow. :) We can make it fun as possible. I'll have a blast this summer just being out, no school, hot weather, friends. Here we come, summer!

Sadly, there weren't many "wins" during Natalie's battle. It seemed like every time we saw a glimmer of hope, it was dashed by a worse revelation. I can only imagine the emotional roller coaster Natalie herself must have experienced. Some days she felt pretty good all things considered. Those days offered some semblance of normalcy—watching her favorite TV shows or movies, shopping, and visiting with friends. Other days were horrendous—full of nausea, pain, and doctor visits. Then there were the days that held both—starting out okay but devolving as the hours passed.

All this might not seem a big deal without witnessing firsthand what Natalie's daily life had become. The chemo was brutal. The radiation was draining. The weight gain from the steroids was disturbing. The wheelchair was uncomfortable. Her utter dependence on others to transport her everywhere was frustrating. The bedsores were excruciating. The inability to control her bathroom functions was humiliating. The weekly trips to the doctor were inconvenient. The hospital stays were arduous, physically and emotionally.

Even the weekly visits from the children's hospice staff proved more irritating than helpful. This was part of the hospital's program to offer ongoing support for children coping with serious illness. But Natalie didn't appreciate having to answer the same questions she'd just been asked at her weekly doctor's visit. She longed to just hang out and do regular activities with her friends. Go to school. Play softball. But between the medical appointments, chemo, and administration of at least half a dozen drugs each day, her little body was worn out. And that was on a good week when she had no bedsores or vomiting to contend with.

Still, Natalie kept a smile on her face and never wavered in her belief that she could be fully healed. She insisted on participating as much as possible in normal activities. She loved watching Will's baseball games and getting her nacho fix from the concession stand. Talking on the phone was draining. How do you respond to friends reporting their fun activities while you lie in bed all day? But she did enjoy texting them.

She also watched her softball team's games, though it was hard not to be on the field with them. Her teammates and coaches showed their love and support by stitching her name on their ballcaps and holding a fundraiser for her.

As her disease continuously brought new challenges, Natalie adjusted her view of what a good life is to the reality of her current situation. Though frequently nauseated, in pain, and fatigued, she resisted making everyone else around her miserable. She maintained her sense of humor and chose laughter over hurt and bitterness. She still managed to find joy in the moment. She epitomized the wise words of King Solomon:

A cheerful heart is good medicine, but a broken spirit saps a person's strength. (Proverbs 17:22, NLT)

Natalie could also find the funny side in any situation. She and Tom had some comical adventures throughout this journey. Now that she was bedridden, a common entertainment was watching some of her favorite movies. Her television was an older model, so Tom took her to the store to buy a new one that would play DVDs. They'd barely pulled into the store parking lot when a torrential downpour started. Pulling up to the curb, Tom lifted her out of the car, then rolled her wheelchair into the front lobby so she could wait there out of the rain while he parked the car.

I'm sure people walking by must have gawked at the pudgy girl in the wheelchair and wondered why her caregivers had abandoned her there. Others may have formed false opinions about her health issues based on her weight gain and accompanying "moon face," as we experienced many times throughout her illness. I'm sure it bothered her to be sitting alone in public watching the look on people's faces as they passed her. But she later recounted the incident to my mom with typical humor. "Ma-Maw, if I'd just had a [begging] cup, I could have made some money!"

During an extended hospital stay in September, the doctors inserted an internal feeding tube into Natalie's abdomen to keep her nourished since she could no longer keep food down. Her first week at home, she was relaxing in her favorite recliner when she needed to go to the bathroom. Tom picked her up, but he failed to notice that the long tube was still wedged in the recliner. As he started to move down the hallway, Natalie yelled, "The tube is stuck in the chair!"

She started laughing as the tube came loose from her body. Tom was mortified since the tube couldn't just be shoved back inside of her like a retractable tape measure. He called me, a bit freaked out.

I tried to contain my laughter. "Why are you calling me? I have no idea what to do to correct that. You're going to have to call the gastroenterologist."

While I was equally concerned about eating complications or infection, I couldn't imagine this was the first time something like that had happened with a feeding tube. Sure enough, when Tom called, the gastroenterologist told him to bring Natalie in the next day and he'd fix the problem. The mishap turned out to be a blessing in disguise because the doctor was able to replace the tube with a much simpler device called a Mic-Key. Natalie's ability to laugh rather than freaking out at one more thing going wrong helped diffuse an alarming situation.

While a good laugh didn't totally alleviate our sadness, it did give us an occasional break from it. Instead of being grouchy when Tom woke her each morning to administer her meds, Natalie would pull her covers up over her head and say with a chuckle, "Don't wake the princess! She's not ready to get up yet."

Natalie's willingness to find humor amidst the muck and mire made the hardest days more bearable. Her resilience pushed her to exhaust every effort to beat the disease. Her focus may have shifted to the day-to-day goal of surviving a deadly illness, but she lived each day with the same zest for success as she did when she was well. She was a living example of the apostle James' challenge:

Dear brothers and sisters, when troubles of any kind come your way, consider it an opportunity for great joy. (James 1:2, NLT)

Let me make clear here that I'm not diminishing the situation. This was the worst year of our lives. There's so much truth to the saying, "As a mother, you are only as happy as your saddest child." It was heart-wrenching to see our daughter suffer so greatly and know we couldn't alleviate her discomfort. No human should have to experience that degree of demoralization, especially a child.

Natalie had expressed interest in being a pediatrician. She was still young, and interests change, but it hurt knowing she'd likely never realize any of her hopes and dreams. I hated watching her goals shift from long-term aspirations of marriage and medical school to simply surviving each day. We should be shopping together, going to her softball games, and navigating adolescent girl issues. Not determining what medication would stop the health issue of the day, relying on others to feed us, or figuring out how to be involved in Will's life without causing more distress for her.

I've never felt so powerless and was simply shocked on many days that this was what our lives had become. As time passed, I could scarcely see how anything good could come out of the prolonged agony my little girl was suffering. I didn't want to lose her, but I also didn't want her to have to live like this. Tom and I would willingly have traded places with her, and I often asked God, *Why can't this be me instead of her?* In truth, I was deeply disappointed that this was the plan God had chosen for my daughter's life.

For Will, too, it was tough to watch his vibrant little sister become more and more incapacitated. But regardless of all that seemed to go wrong, neither Tom and I nor Will nor even Natalie herself blamed God or wavered in our trust that he understood the bigger plan for her life and our family. God never promised we'd have a life free of difficulties. In fact, Jesus himself assured us that we'd face trouble in this world. But he also promised his peace in the midst of those troubles and trials:

> I have told you all this so that you may have peace in me. Here on earth you will have many trials and sorrows. But take heart because I have overcome the world. (John 16:33, NLT)

Despite the horror of watching cancer gradually destroy our child's body, I didn't feel then—nor do I feel now looking back—that this was a chaotic time for our family. We asked for help when we needed it and took things one day at a time. We hoped and prayed for the best for her each day. Some days, such as when there was a never-ending cycle of medical issues, felt hopeless. Others actually felt somewhat normal. Those were the days when Natalie whined about not liking what was on the menu or the choices we made about how to dress her.

There were certainly far more setbacks with her health than positive developments, so it felt most days like a dark cloud surrounded us. But in all of this, Natalie was a bright light. People consistently commented on her smile and willingness to embrace each moment rather than griping about things she couldn't change. That's quite a feat for anyone, much less a young girl. Natalie simply loved being on the go, and she didn't allow cancer to stop her!

## HELPS SECTION

# *The Rest of the Family*

When one family member is gravely ill, it is easy to make them and their needs the sole focus of daily life. But they are not the only ones going through trauma. It is crucial not to lose sight of the other children or spouse and their needs while ensuring the best care for the sick family member. Here are a few important principles we've learned along the way.

- **Keep the lines of communication open with your other children.** We talked with Will about what was happening to his sister. While we didn't burden him with every detail, we didn't hide any concerns with her condition. We also encouraged him to express how he was feeling.

- **Don't neglect your other children.** We stayed involved with Will's activities and made a conscious effort to have one parent at home in the mornings and evenings during Natalie's hospital stays. We often worried about Will feeling left out, so we tried to arrange or encourage outings that were separate from those he participated in with Natalie. My parents occasionally took Will to lunch and offered him their undivided attention.

- **Don't neglect your spouse.** With the stress Natalie's illness placed on our family, it was important for Tom and me to talk regularly and spend time together just the two of us. This not only helped with decision-making but allowed us to lean on each other when one of us was feeling down. Since

Tom was the only one who could lift and carry Natalie, he was up a lot at night tending to her physical needs. This was not only physically but mentally and emotionally draining. I sat with Natalie every evening which allowed him some time to himself.

## 11

# i can't fix this

"'You will not succeed by your own strength
or by your own power, but by my Spirit,'
says the LORD All-Powerful."
—Zechariah 4:6 (NCV)

On August 23, Natalie had chemotherapy. The side effects made her feel even worse than usual, and three days later she was hospitalized for nonstop vomiting. She was eventually released, only to be readmitted a week later when the vomiting started again. We hadn't seen her this sick since our ordeal began six months prior. Natalie wrote in her journal:

The past week has been pretty awful. On Tuesday, chemo didn't go well at all. I was the most nauseous and sick I've ever been.

It's hard to accurately describe the level of anguish and helplessness I felt as I lay next to my daughter in her hospital bed, watching her vomit bile into a tray because she had nothing else left in her stomach. Tom stayed at the hospital 24/7 so she'd always have someone with her. I'd bring him a change of clothes when I came to see them each morning on my way to work. Tom showered in Natalie's bathroom and only left her side when she had a visitor and to eat dinner once I arrived each evening.

Between my own hospital visits and work, I got Will off to school, made sure he had dinner when he got home from practice, and came home each night to stay with him. This was our routine every weekday. On weekends, Will and I would go to the hospital together so he could spend time with his sister.

Natalie had been in the hospital almost a month with no resolution to the vomiting when one of her doctors pulled me into the hallway to suggest the vomiting was "all in her head." I've never wanted to hit a person so badly. Flabbergasted he'd even suggest such a thing, I responded indignantly, "Why don't you lie here with her for a while and then tell me it's all in her head!"

I wasn't just angry but starting to lose confidence in the hospital staff. Why was it taking so long to figure out what was wrong with my baby?

One Sunday night as I was leaving, Natalie became unusually clingy. To comfort her, I offered, "I'll be back tomorrow, honey, I promise, just as soon as I get Will off to school."

My assurance seemed to settle her down. But during my drive home, she called me, sobbing. "Please take me home! I don't want to stay here anymore!"

I tried to calm Natalie before asking her to put her daddy on the phone. Then I suggested to Tom that we speak with the doctor and request Natalie's release first thing the next morning. After all, if they couldn't diagnose her problem, she might as well be at home with us while we kept on trying to figure out the cause of her vomiting.

The doctor obliged, and we brought Natalie home. Two days later, she had a follow-up appointment with the gastroenterologist who'd inserted her feeding tube. He conducted a CT scan (a computerized X-ray imaging procedure) and immediately determined the vomiting was caused by ulcers in her esophagus, which were a by-product of the chemo.

We were grateful to know the cause and that our daughter might finally experience some relief. But I was infuriated that she'd spent a month in pure misery—and undergoing every test imaginable—while this doctor had been able to diagnose her problem with a single test. It made me question how deeply the hospital had really probed to find the cause or whether they'd just settled for managing her symptoms.

Natalie was taken off chemo to allow healing in her esophagus. At least we were back home together as a family, which left Natalie and all of us in a much better emotional state. Will especially had only been able to visit Natalie on weekends due to his school and baseball schedule. So they were happy to see more of each other again.

But for me this was a very disheartening period, my mind consumed with concern for both my children. *My youngest child's quality of life is continually deteriorating despite our best efforts! Meanwhile, my oldest child is having to experience life without the caliber of attention he deserves from his mom and dad!*

We'd been offered one glimmer of hope during Natalie's September hospital stay. An MRI showed evidence the chemo might be having a positive effect on the tumor. While it hadn't shrunk, neither had it grown, and there was no longer any swelling at the top. The unknown was that there was still swelling at the base of the tumor. This could be caused by the radiation treatments since we were still in that window. But another option was that the tumor might be dying since they typically swell at the bottom before they die.

The oncologist explained that if we saw no change or decrease in Natalie's neurological functions, then the tumor was likely dying. We wouldn't know for six to eight weeks when another MRI could be done. We were cautiously optimistic, but it was hard to be overly hopeful as we witnessed day by day just how miserable Natalie was feeling. Rather than improving or even plateauing as the oncologist hoped, she seemed to be on a consistently downward spiral.

And yet Natalie herself appeared surprisingly unafraid. On October 9 while lying in bed late one night, she used her cell phone to record herself singing a popular praise song by the Christian contemporary music group Hillsong called "Mighty to Save." The lyrics speak of God's power to save as well as his compassion, love, and mercy. More pertinently, they speak of Jesus conquering death through his resurrection from the grave.

The following day, Natalie texted me the audio file. I still treasure that recording and marvel that when she was alone so late at night with no one to put on a good face for or any other positive pretense, her own choice was to praise and worship her heavenly Father. Knowing that's what she had on her mind and in her heart so close to the end of her life continues to give me comfort.

One late October Saturday, I sensed for the first time that Natalie knew death was drawing near. She'd never made any reference to dying until that day, but while we were watching television, she casually asked, "When I die, can I be buried between you and Daddy?"

The topic of burials isn't something a child her age normally even considers, and it crushed me that she was pondering such a somber thought. Caught off guard, I responded instinctively, "Oh, Nat! You're going to want to be buried next to your future husband, not between your old parents."

But I was left wondering if deep inside she knew her body was shutting down. Especially when she asked just a short time later, "Mommy, can we say that prayer together I prayed with you when I got saved?"

She was referring to what's known as the Sinner's—or Salvation—Prayer, a simple prayer that can be found in many evangelistic pamphlets or even at the end of a Bible or hymnbook, designed for a person to pray when they wish to start or renew a personal relationship with God through his Son Jesus Christ. Natalie had prayed a child's version of the prayer when she accepted Jesus as her Savior at the age of ten. Her request now seemed to come out of nowhere, but I assumed she just wanted assurance about her eternal destination, so we bowed our heads together and prayed the prayer.

By now Natalie's thirteenth birthday was approaching. She wanted to celebrate with her friends and see the latest release of her favorite movie franchise—a musical about a group of high school friends. On Saturday, October 25, nine twelve-year-old girls came over for cake. We then ventured out to the theater for the third movie in the series. Natalie wasn't feeling well because her ulcers had still not healed, but she enjoyed having friends around. The girls were so loving and nurturing toward her, and it was clear to me she'd made wise choices with her friendships.

The next day she still didn't feel well, but she worked on her homework anyway. We were proud of Natalie for pushing through and always keeping up with her seventh-grade schoolwork. But we also wanted her to feel like her birthday week was an escape from the drudgery of her daily routine. Tom took her to one of her favorite childhood hangouts that offered pizza and games. They had a blast as evidenced by her joyous smile in the black and white photo booth pictures they brought home.

November 1 was Natalie's actual birthday. A friend had offered to pamper Natalie and one of her friends that afternoon at her salon. So she and her closest friend, Sydney, rode to the salon in a limousine for manicures, pedicures, and cake.

"I feel like a princess!" she exclaimed to us when she got home.

That was such a good day! These joyful moments seemed few and far between, but we all relished the brief respite and had no idea then how important those few weekends of quality time with friends and family would become. God, who knows what lies ahead, had gone before us to bless our girl in a special way.

In her own human strength, Natalie tried her best to look beyond her discouraging circumstances. But it was to her heavenly Father that she clung for the strength to endure each day. In her November 2 journal entry, she wrote:

Thank goodness the ulcers are healed! I'm so glad we got that taken care of. Although I'm really not looking forward to starting chemo again. I guess we'll find out on Tuesday when I go back to the doctor where we go next. I have been eating a little dinner most nights. I haven't found myself to be as hungry lately. And all of it has stayed down for about the past week or so. So, we're moving along and getting somewhere. Thanks be to God! He truly is an awesome God!

Natalie trusted God, and people noticed. Around this time, we were contacted by a local author who had heard about Natalie through a mutual friend. He asked Natalie to write a paragraph about strength for a book he was writing on women and girls overcoming adversity. Puzzled, she asked, "What do I know about strength?"

*Are you kidding me?* I can remember thinking. *You're the poster child for strength!*

Natalie had just learned about acrostic verses, so I suggested she use that approach to capture her thoughts. Here is what she sent me later that day:

### Strength

*Striving to go on no matter what.*
*Trusting God to carry you through tough times.*
*Reminding yourself you can do anything you set your mind to.*
*Enjoying every moment of life, no matter how hard it gets.*
*Never giving up.*
*Giving all you've got.*
*Toughness to move on and fight 'til the end.*
*Having the courage and might to battle through anything.*

Natalie was scheduled later that week for a full-body MRI. We were eager to get it done as we'd finally know the outcome of the lower swelling observed on the previous test in September—i.e., whether the tumor was actually dying or not. Natalie's appointment was Thursday morning, which required fasting before the procedure. We'd been unaware that her IV fluids counted as food intake, so we were told to come back the next day. What made the delay even more disappointing was that her test would now be on a Friday, which meant waiting anxiously for the results until the following Monday rather than hearing them the next day.

When we arrived at the clinic on Monday, November 10, Natalie was whisked off for blood work while Tom and I were asked to join her doctor in the conference room. We knew what that meant, so our hearts immediately sank. With the decline we'd seen in Natalie over the past several weeks, I can't honestly say I expected good news. But I'd fought continuously against my natural pessimism and pushed myself to maintain hope. I knew God was bigger than all of this. If he chose, he could miraculously heal our daughter's broken earthly body right up to the moment she took her last breath.

Natalie's oncologist walked in with Sharon, our Family Life Specialist. They both looked solemn as they took their seats across the table from Tom and me. The oncologist's tone was compassionate but blunt as he explained the test results. "The MRI shows the tumor has grown one centimeter down and two centimeters up into her brain stem [which controls her breathing and heart-rate]. Natalie likely has no more than four to six weeks to live."

His devastating statement caught me totally off guard. We'd left his office in September trying to temper our expectations but hopeful the tumor might be dying. So we were simply not prepared for a blow of this magnitude. *This is so much worse than I ever anticipated! Our girl isn't going to live to see another Christmas!*

All restraint exhausted, Tom and I both grabbed tissues from the table as we broke into anguished sobbing. But the doctor still had one small gray area of hope to hold out. He told us about an experimental drug which had achieved a mild level of success. But once he explained that the drug had shown promise with just one child, extending his life by just a few months, Tom and I both felt our daughter had been through enough. It would be selfish to simply prolong her misery.

The doctor encouraged us to let Natalie have a say in the matter. She'd asked a lot of intelligent questions at her weekly checkups and shown she understood what was happening with her body. He felt she was capable of weighing the options to help make the decision. Tom and I prayed for wisdom right there in the conference room, and God gave us the peace to allow Natalie to decide.

We joined Natalie in the examination room. Sitting down in a chair across from her, the doctor leaned forward to say gently and kindly, "Natalie, this disease is going to take your life."

She immediately put her hands to her face and burst into tears. Up to that point, it was the worst moment of my entire life. Words cannot convey how badly my heart ached to see my daughter so devastated.

But the oncologist quickly pivoted to the clinical trial. He explained what was involved then asked Natalie what she thought. Looking him straight in the eye, she said quietly, "I want to try. I want to live."

My heart broke that day in a way I will never recover from. I am a fixer by nature, but I couldn't fix this. Our baby was going to die, and there was nothing I could do to protect her from it.

On our way home from the clinic, Natalie asked, "Can we go watch Sydney's softball game?"

Her request amazed me. I would have gone home, curled up in a ball, and sobbed. But Natalie still wanted to experience life—normal life—even if only for a few hours. That night when Tom was putting her to bed, she reached up, grabbed Tom's face, and pulled him close.

"Thank you for taking care of me, Daddy," she said, kissing him. In hindsight, I wondered if she felt she needed to say it then. Did she know her time was running out and wanted to make sure her daddy understood how much she appreciated all he'd done for her?

That had to be the worst day of our precious little daughter's existence. I'm not sure how I'd react if my doctor had just told me I was at the end of my young life. Mortality isn't a natural part of our thinking at that age. But Natalie pressed on as she noted in her journal:

> I will continue to fight this battle to the end. It will NOT defeat me. I WILL defeat it. Nothing will bring me down. The LORD is my rock.

I see such beauty in the way God designed Natalie with the necessary traits *"for such a time as this"* (Esther 4:14). Her innate qualities—while they could be exasperating at times as her parent—served her well, forming a strong, faith-filled young lady who remained steadfast in her trust in God and refused to give up in the face of adversity. Well-known nineteenth century British preacher Charles Spurgeon once said, "Trials teach us what we are; they dig up the soil and let us see what we are made of."[3]

This was certainly true of Natalie. Even knowing the cancer had moved into her brain stem and that without a miracle her remaining days were limited, she radiated a sense of peace rather than a spirit of fear. Deep inside, she understood she was a winner either way. She'd either remain here with us or she'd be in the presence of Jesus in heaven.

HELPS SECTION

# Safe-Guarding Emotional Well-Being

Daily life doesn't come to an end when a family member has been diagnosed with a life-threatening illness. Creating a home environment that is as comfortable and close to normal as their condition allows is vital to their ongoing emotional well-being and helps a sick child feel like a normal kid, even if just for a little while. Here are just a few ideas that were of benefit to us.

- **Let them express their feelings in a manner that's comfortable for them.** Remaining positive is important, but they also need freedom to honestly express negative feelings, fears, and concerns for the future. Natalie used her written words to communicate her thoughts and feelings. Her outlets were journaling on the CaringBridge site, texting on her cell phone, and writing to her pen pal Jessie. When it came to talking on the phone, she wanted only to talk with Tom and me. Allow your loved-one to determine what their outlet is and then offer them the tools they need.

- **Encourage them to find activities that bring them joy.** This offers a respite from the reality of their daily life. Natalie liked to draw, play games, watch movies, and play a popular computer game.

- **Allow friends to come over.** Natalie felt especially isolated once she was no longer in school. Encouraging and even arranging for friends to spend time with your loved-one helps them regain some form of normalcy. When they can't have visitors, connecting with friends through texts, e-mails, video chats, phone calls, or social media sites can help them stay upbeat.

- **Special activities and outings that break up the sameness of each day are also a welcome distraction.** Since Natalie loved making things, her friends would bring craft projects to the house and work on them with her. Going on walks, riding in her golf cart, or taking trips to the mall provided a welcome change of scenery. Natalie's friend, Geneva, even invited her to watch a movie at a nearby theater.

# a devastating loss

"Don't let your hearts be troubled. Trust in God, and trust also in me. There is more than enough room in my Father's home. If this were not so, would I have told you that I am going to prepare a place for you? When everything is ready, I will come and get you, so that you will always be with me where I am. And you know the way to where I am going."
—John 14:1-4 (NLT)

I've often heard that dogs can sense things even humans can't. Everyone in our family deeply loved our adorable Miniature Dachshund Tucker. But Natalie had a particularly strong attachment to him, constantly carrying him around or snuggling with him on the sofa while she watched her favorite TV shows or read a book.

So it was both difficult and strange to see how Tucker would no longer jump into her lap as her health deteriorated. I wondered if he knew Natalie was dying and wanted to detach himself. Or maybe he sensed she was fragile and was afraid he might hurt her.

It broke my heart when Natalie saw it too. "Mommy, Tucker won't stay in my lap. He keeps jumping off."

I continued to lift Tucker to her lap, but he would immediately jump down. A place where he'd once found great comfort was now undesirable. It hurt Natalie's feelings that he no longer wanted to snuggle with her, and it became yet another source of her joy stripped away by this disease.

But despite hurt feelings and all her physical limitations, Natalie still found enjoyment in getting out of the house. Over the next two weeks, she participated in a number of outings. She came for lunch at my office with Tom and Will, where she clowned around with my phones, and was smiling and chatty. She visited her cousins and enjoyed going to the salon each Saturday to have her hair washed and blown dry.

As late as one week before her death, she went to church. We were able to have a family picture taken there, the last we have. My eyes tear up remembering her plea to cover her wheelchair with a rug so the photo would look "normal like our others."

After church, we took Natalie to her favorite pancake house for lunch. That may have been the last meal she could fully enjoy as her ability to swallow was diminishing quickly.

Despite her determination, Natalie was still human, and she felt both scared and discouraged. She captured her thoughts in an e-mail exchange with her math teacher just five days before she passed away.

**From Her Teacher:**

Hi, Favorite Student :)!

I haven't talked to you since all of the birthday festivities, so thought I would drop you a line. I visited your CaringBridge site and saw that you've started more chemo. Please remember that I'm rooting for you every step of the way. You are my hero in more ways than you know. Every night, I keep you tucked safely in my prayers. Hang in there! Hugs galore … Ms. V

**Natalie's Response:**

Thank you so much. They're not as positive as I was hoping as it is experimental and not many have received it. But I'm going for it. I promised myself I wasn't ever giving up, ever. I went Monday and go back tomorrow, Thursday. I have infusions twice a week.

I've now got a terrible cold. My weak immune system is trying to fight it off. I'm on sooo very many medications. I am having a lot of trouble breathing. When I try to eat, I end up choking. It is very scary. I'm getting nervous as the tumor has grown also up into my brain stem. I just take it moment by moment and thank God for every day I am blessed with. Must stand strong!

On Saturday, November 22, we began seeing a drastic change in Natalie. She asked to get her hair washed at the salon, but afterward we could see her energy level was waning. We'd made plans for dinner at a favorite restaurant with my younger brother and his family. We offered to cancel, but she wanted to see her cousins, so we went ahead. The entire evening, she sat next to me with her head resting on my shoulder. I kept my arm around her, stroking her hair. She barely touched her food and looked so tired and frail I wondered if we were getting close to the end. I learned afterwards that the inability to swallow is symptomatic of the body shutting down.

The next day, Sunday, November 23, Natalie and I were lying in her bed watching our hometown football team, the Carolina Panthers, play the Atlanta Falcons. She was still very lethargic and complained that her collar bone hurt. She could no longer hold on when Tom picked her up to carry her, and we thought perhaps trying to keep a grip was placing a strain on her collar bone. She'd already lost control of her lower body. Now she was losing all remaining strength in both hands.

We called her doctor, and he prescribed another medication. But it did little good. Even texting on her cell phone—her favorite escape outlet—was becoming more difficult. Tom and I were alarmed as we realized the progression of the tumor up her spine was now affecting the dexterity of her arm and hand movements just as it had with her legs. I stayed in bed with Natalie all day just to be close to her.

By this stage, Natalie had developed what is called a death rattle, which sounded as though she was congested but it was actually because the air no longer flowed properly to her lungs. Speaking had become increasingly difficult, especially trying to form consonants, so it was hard to understand her. One of Natalie's cousins, a teacher, had set up a whiteboard with the alphabet on it. This allowed Natalie to communicate by pointing to letters to spell out words.

Later that day, the local author who had asked Natalie to write about strength stopped by for a visit. He was kind, and she was quiet. He later captured their encounter in his book *Voice of Beauty*.

### *A Beautiful Battle*

While working on this book, a friend drew my attention to a young girl battling for her life in my hometown. Natalie was 13-years-old [she was actually twelve] when diagnosed with cancer. Although she would not make it to her fourteenth birthday, she decided to spend her final days pouring out smiles and words of encouragement to those around her. One Sunday afternoon, I had the privilege of meeting Natalie and sharing my desire to honor her in *Voice of Beauty*. As her tired face struggled to generate a smile, I recognized the beauty and strength that her friends, family, and nurses had told me she portrayed. When I heard of her death two days later, I reflected on her life as I watched the vibrant leaves float to the ground. Like autumn's foliage, God often makes people look most beautiful at the brink of death.[4]

That was a rough day for Natalie and an even rougher night. Tom was up with her most of the night. The next morning, November 24, was the Monday before Thanksgiving. Though scheduled to work that day, I woke up feeling I needed to stay home, especially after Natalie's difficult weekend. Tom told me she'd had a bad night and was too sore to move. She was scheduled for chemo at ten-thirty that morning, so we called the oncologist's office and explained how she was feeling. The doctor told us to go ahead and bring her in but to take our time until she felt up to it.

We finally arrived at noon. Her oncologist informed us he was canceling the chemo. He'd wanted to do an MRI, but after listening to Natalie's breathing, he determined it was pointless to put her through that since it would only confirm what he already knew. He'd identified shadows on the brain from the previous MRI, and it was now clear the tumor had infiltrated those areas of the brain.

The oncologist went on to tell us Natalie had only two to seven days left to live. I literally had no words. Another piece of my battered, bruised heart was chipped away, and all I could do was pray.

We stayed at the oncology clinic while the medical staff made Natalie comfortable on morphine so we could take her home. Being at the hospital always upset her, so we wanted her to be at home when she passed away. Bad from the start, the day got progressively worse. Our little girl was dying right in front of us. Tom and I took turns walking out of the room to cry.

I was sitting at Natalie's bedside, watching her breathe, when my phone buzzed. Looking down, I saw an e-mail from a colleague. Attached was a list of comments from my ministry teammates expressing why they were thankful for me. It was something we did each year at Thanksgiving, and God knew I needed the encouragement at that exact moment.

As we loaded Natalie back into the car, I pleaded with God to take her home quickly rather than prolonging her misery for days. It is simply impossible to describe in words how it feels to see your daughter's body shutting down like that. I had a battle going on in my mind about which made me a worse parent—wanting to selfishly keep her here trapped in a shell of a life and body or wanting her suffering to finally stop.

Even then, Natalie remained hopeful. Despite the morphine and death rattle, she was trying her best to communicate. On our way home, she let us know that once she felt better, she wanted to shop for a new cell phone with a larger keyboard that would be easier to manipulate with her feeble fingers. Her body might have been giving out, but her mind and spirit weren't giving up.

Once home, we got Natalie settled in her own bed. Her favorite hospice nurse arrived, and he got her pain regulated with three milli-grams of morphine every ten minutes. The atmosphere was heavy—just a feeling of hopelessness and deep sadness. No one really talked much. Then her nurse pulled us aside and asked if we'd said our goodbyes.

"We've told her how much we love her and how proud we are of her," I said. "But we don't want her to think we are giving up hope,"

He shook his head in disagreement. "Many times when people are dying, they hold onto life for the sake of their loved-ones. You should tell her that you are at peace with her letting go."

The nurse's words hung in the air as we stood around Natalie, mon-itoring her comfort level. Suddenly, Natalie started pointing toward the corner of her bedroom where a hospital-grade bed had been brought in months earlier when we were dealing with her bedsores. Tom had been sleeping there so he wouldn't have to run up and down stairs each night. None of us could understand what she was trying to tell us.

"Nat, what do you want?" Tom and I chorused. "Do you want to move over there?"

We were perplexed since she'd always hated that bed. But Natalie continued to point in that direction, so Tom and I with the help of the hospice nurse gently moved her to the hospital bed. Once settled there, she reached out her hand several times. Tom attempted to hold it, but each time she shook him off.

Tom looked over at me. "I think she wants you."

I took her hand in mine, but she shook me off too. When she started fidgeting, we opted to move her back to her own bed. It was such an odd encounter, but we finally got her settled and comfortable.

At this same time, I was feeling panicked that we still hadn't chosen a place for a burial. I'd visited numerous cemeteries once the doctors had made clear the inevitability of Natalie's passing, but none felt right. I'd heard once that you'll know if you want to buy a home within the first nine seconds after entering it. That's how I felt about the cemeteries I'd visited. None of them felt like the place I wanted to bury my child.

I also wanted a headstone for Natalie. I don't know why. I just wanted my girl to have her name above ground where people would see it. Few cemeteries in our city allow headstones due to space issues. Tom and I had an appointment the next day to visit the last option on my list. After what we'd heard at the oncology clinic, I didn't feel it could wait.

A close friend drove me to the family-owned cemetery, which was about twenty minutes from our home. I hadn't realized the cemetery was part of a full-service funeral home. My friend and I climbed into the funeral director's car. She drove us across the street to where the cemetery was located and through the grounds to the available plots.

I spotted a beautifully green area nestled between two trees and close to a sidewalk where anyone walking by could see it. The moment I saw it, I knew this was the right place for my daughter. The environment was quiet and serene, and we could place a bench next to one of the trees for reflective visits. I'd finally found the inner peace I'd been seeking.

Natalie had been concerned earlier that I was leaving the house, so my friend and I didn't linger. I made a down payment to the funeral home, then headed home. A few hours later, Will arrived home from school. I explained what was going on.

"We took Nat to the clinic today, and the doctor told us she will likely only live another two to seven days. You should sit with her and use this opportunity to tell her whatever it is you want or need to say."

Will went upstairs to sit with Natalie and say his goodbyes. Meanwhile, I ran out to the drugstore to get her some medication for her congestion. The whole way there and back, I prayed that God would please take her quickly. I couldn't bear to watch her agonize much longer.

We'd set up a baby monitor by Natalie's bed to keep an ear out for her when we were out of the room. When I walked back into the house, I could hear Will on the monitor telling Natalie what she meant to him and that she was his best friend. His words shredded whatever was left of my heart. I'd watched over the years as God faithfully honored my prayers that my son and daughter be close friends, and hearing the anguish in my son's voice was almost more than I could bear.

When it sounded as though Will was wrapping up his thoughts, I went upstairs to join them. Will was sitting beside Natalie's bed, holding her left hand, so I lay down beside her and held her right hand. Soon after, Tom joined us.

Choking back my tears, I told my precious daughter, "Nat, you've done more for the Lord in thirteen years than most do in eighty. It's okay to go be with Jesus. He'll take good care of you."

I meant that with all of my heart. Within five minutes, I looked into her eyes and saw nothing there. They were open, but there was no sparkle, no life.

"I think she's gone," I said through my tears.

Coming closer, Tom checked her pulse. There was none. God is indeed good and merciful, and he took our Natalie quickly to heaven just shy of ten o'clock on that Monday night, November 24, 2008.

# 13

# saying goodbye

"And now, dear brothers and sisters, we want you
to know what will happen to the believers who have died so
you will not grieve like people who have no hope. For since
we believe that Jesus died and was raised to life again,
we also believe that when Jesus returns, God will bring
back with him the believers who have died."
—1 Thessalonians 4:13-14 (NLT)

We called family and friends first, then called the hospice nurse to notify him of Natalie's passing. When he arrived to make final arrangements, he asked me what happened. I filled him in on the events of the evening. He wasn't surprised. Since he is around a lot of children when they die, he'd been pretty certain death was imminent. He went on to explain that earlier in the day when Natalie was pointing toward the hospital bed, he thought she was trying to tell us she'd seen Jesus or an angel in that corner of her room.

The hospice nurse also explained, more fully this time, that when people are close to death, they often hang on out of worry for those they're leaving behind. When I told Natalie it was okay to go with Jesus, this was the first time we'd let her know we were at peace with her leaving us. Prior to that, we were always concerned she'd feel we were giving up hope that she might be healed. Once we gave our blessing to go with Jesus, she'd done just that.

# saying goodbye

Natalie never did show any fear during her last day on earth. Maybe she was just too tired and feeling too sick to show any emotion, but I believe it was because Jesus' presence was with her, soothing and comforting her. It warms my heart as a mom to know that at the time my little girl had every earthly reason to be most afraid, she was calm and at peace.

Our next step was calling the funeral home attached to the cemetery I'd chosen earlier that day. When their personnel showed up a little later, I witnessed the most beautiful encounter. Tom asked if he could bring Natalie downstairs instead of them coming to get her. He'd carried her around for months, and this was the last time he'd ever get to do it.

I will never forget how tenderly Tom carried his little girl down the stairs, the anguish written all over his face. It was like he was afraid he was going to hurt her. Despite the pain and grief, it was the sweetest moment, and I wasn't sure he was going to be able to let her go.

The next morning, I just felt numb. Everything had gone downhill so quickly there'd been no time to fully wrap my head around it. Tom and I had an appointment with the funeral home to pick out a casket, but it all felt somewhat mechanical—like I was going down the list and checking boxes. I'd always expected that one day I might have to pick out a casket for my parents or Tom. That at age forty-four I'd be selecting one for our daughter felt surreal.

I understood that a casket is a box that will go into the ground, never to be seen again. But I also wanted our princess to have a beautiful resting place. Blue was Natalie's favorite color, so we settled on a light-blue casket with white silk lining that was simple yet elegant in design—much like Natalie's own taste. She always wanted to dress nice but without all the accessories so as to not draw attention to herself.

While still at the funeral home, I received a text from my employer offering our organization's main meeting hall as a place for Natalie's celebration of life. With the outpouring of support we'd experienced throughout Natalie's illness, Tom and I had been concerned our church might not accommodate all those wanting to pay tribute. So this was a huge answer to prayer and blessing before we'd even asked!

Our next stop was a meeting with our pastor to plan the funeral program. During the past nine-plus months, we'd never allowed our thoughts to gravitate to planning a funeral. Hope always overruled practicality. Though not an easy task, it was oddly comforting to choose Natalie's favorite praise songs and scripture passages. I could visualize her singing these favorites at church and in the car.

We celebrated—if you could call it that—Thanksgiving a few days later. That was my first taste of emptiness. I hadn't realized how painful it would be to gather among family and see the glaring omission at the table. When Natalie's closest girl cousin, Bailey, entered the room, it just seemed that Natalie should be standing next to her. That's the way it had always been. I didn't realize at the time that this angst was creating a new normal for me. It was simply too painful to be around family without my daughter.

Friends had been in and out of our home all week, caring for our physical needs. We'd scheduled the funeral visitation, when family and friends could say their goodbyes to Natalie, for Friday evening at the funeral home. This was the first time Tom, Will, and I had seen Natalie since she'd left our house on Monday, and it was gut-wrenching. Though dressed in her favorite outfit, this wasn't our girl but a pale, cold shell. Our Natalie was gone.

Tom, Will, and I each spent a few tearful moments with Natalie. For Will, I could only imagine what it felt like seeing your only sibling lying lifeless in a casket. Then together we tucked Natalie's favorite stuffed animal Bear, a patchwork mix of pastel colors, under her right arm. Natalie had loved Bear since she was old enough to crawl over and grab him out of her toy basket. In fact, she loved Bear so much she wouldn't let him travel anywhere outside our home for fear he'd be lost.

One summer when Natalie was five years old, she'd been invited to spend the night with her cousin at my parents' house. She was hesitant to go because she was fearful of getting homesick, but she really wanted to hang out with her favorite cousin. To alleviate homesickness, I suggested she take Bear.

I will never forget her dismay at my solution. "Mommy, if Bear got lost, how could I sleep at night?"

I had no good answer for that question, so I took her to the store, where she picked out a stuffed white-and-black cow—which affectionately became known as Molly Moo Cow—to take to the sleepover at Pa-Paw and Ma-Maw's. Poor Bear never got to leave the confines of Natalie's room, but Molly got to go on vacations and sleepovers. I couldn't imagine burying Natalie without Bear by her side. Molly Moo Cow had always played second fiddle to Bear, but she deserved to be with our girl too, so we tucked her under Natalie's left arm.

Will had one other contribution to tuck in at Natalie's side. He'd let us make a copy of the letter he'd written to his sister, and rereading it after all of these years, I remain struck by the maturity of his thoughts. As a teenager, he already understood the real possibility that the memory of his deep love for his sister might fade with time.

Dear Natalie,

I know there is no way for me to express in the words we have here on earth how much I love you and will miss you. I'm very happy you're in heaven and that you don't have any more pain. I'm also glad to know I'll see you again. You lived one amazing life while you were here. I guess it doesn't matter to you anymore that your life was so short, even though it definitely stinks for us and the world. I say the world because you made a great impact on other people besides your family. Shorty, I and so many people know that you let the Lord live through you. God must be extremely proud of you, and you must have a ton of crowns to throw at Jesus's feet. Thank you for always smiling throughout your illness, and thank you for showing how greatly God can be leaned upon in tough times. The most thanks goes to God, of course, for creating you and blessing us with you. But my greatest thanks is for your life before cancer. Thanks for being my little sister. You were my best friend, the person I could connect with in a deeper way than my friends from school or other places. I think God gave us a special relationship (I should say I know). I will try my hardest, and with the Lord's help, I will remember how much I loved you. Of course, I still love you (you probably already understood what I'm trying to say, but I'll explain myself anyway). What I mean is I want to remember the deep, sincere love that God instilled in me (and many others) during the days before you got sick. During the days we went to Hawaii, the beach, and other vacations, the "normal" days after school when we got to be brother and sister, the weekends, the summers, the holidays, and other days I'm forgetting right now. Those are the days where I can find the love that was so special while you were here. I guess all I have to say now is thank you for being a wonderful sister, and I want to thank the Lord for loving all of his children and for having a plan for all of us, and for him including you in his plan for me and many others. Thanks for watching over us now. I hope you are honored today, Nat, and I hope God is also honored. I love you Nat.

Love, your brother and friend,
Willy

Our private time with Natalie was now over. Kissing my daughter's cold forehead, I spoke silently to her one last time. *Rest in peace, my sweet baby!* The rest of our family then joined us to say their goodbyes. Though it was still twenty minutes before the public visitation was scheduled to begin, the funeral director came in to ask if we could start early because the line of visitors was already wrapping around their building.

What an amazing tribute to our girl that so many people loved her! It helped give us the stamina we needed to push through the evening. The receiving of friends was scheduled to last three hours but took almost four and a half. Many of Natalie's friends came and placed special notes and items in her casket. By the time it was over, we were mentally and emotionally exhausted. But we still had her burial and funeral to face.

We laid our little girl to rest the next morning, Saturday, November 29, 2008, in a private graveside ceremony. We'd only invited immediate family and a few friends who had a special relationship with Natalie. Rain was pouring down, and watching my daughter being lowered into the ground was one of the hardest moments of the hardest week of my life. This was it! I would never again during my life here on this earth lay eyes on my precious baby girl. It brought a sense of finality that was almost more than I could bear.

We stopped at our church for lunch before making our way to my organization's headquarters for Natalie's Celebration of Life. Though we knew a lot of people loved Natalie and our family, this was the Saturday after Thanksgiving, so we weren't sure what turnout to expect. But as it turned out, the meeting hall was packed, and the service was exactly what we'd hoped when planning it. Family, friends, and church leaders our little girl had loved and respected played praise music, sang, preached on her favorite passages, and eulogized her. The ceremony ended with the recording of Natalie singing the Hillsong praise melody "Mighty to Save" that she'd texted me back in October.

It was all a wonderful tribute to a life well lived. But I was still in shock that my daughter was actually gone, and throughout the service I felt like I was functioning on autopilot. I tried to focus only on what was happening at the moment to prevent my thoughts from gravitating to the stark reality of why we were here. This wasn't a church worship service but the final public acknowledgement of my baby's physical existence. The people gathered here to honor my daughter were doing so because she no longer existed here on this earth.

Throughout our nine-and-a-half-month nightmare, God had kept our family calm and focused on him. We trusted God to give us the strength for each day, and we only tackled one day at a time. Natalie's unwavering faith in the face of such adversity was an example for all of us. The fruit of her faith was apparent throughout her suffering. Even toward the end of her life when there was never any positive news, she didn't wallow in self-pity or allow it to dispel her hope for healing.

I can still remember walking into church the day after Natalie's funeral, and the pastor saying to me, "I'm not surprised you all are here. It's who you are."

Actually, it's because of *whose* we are.

## HELPS SECTION

# *Support to Grieving Family*

Continued support for the family is even more crucial once a terminally ill loved-one has passed away, not just immediately after loss, but during the ongoing grieving and healing process.

**In Immediate Aftermath of Loss**

- **Silence is deafening.** Make sure you reach out in some capacity.

- **Send an encouraging note or text** and expect no response.

- **Be present.** Many times, someone's presence alone was sufficient.

- **Listen before you speak.** Try to refrain from offering counsel that could be construed as insensitive or, worse, out of touch.

- **Be prudent in choosing your words.** Avoid platitudes or saying you know how they feel—unless you've experienced what they are going through.

- **Choose scripture verses wisely.** They can be very comforting but can also come across as preachy and self-righteous.

- **Continue to offer practical aid.** The first weeks after a death can be as busy and stressful as during the illness, so cooked meals, cleaning, running errands, lawn services, and other practical support may still be greatly appreciated.

- **Consider holding or contributing to a fundraiser** in memory of the deceased or to help find a cure for illnesses they've been affected by.

- **Pray.**

# 14

# you just get through it

"So we fix our eyes not on what is seen,
but on what is unseen, since what is seen is temporary,
but what is unseen is eternal."
—2 Corinthians 4:18 (NIV)

A friend who had also lost a child once made a poignant statement I've never forgotten. "You never get over the loss of a child. You just get through it."

Those two short sentences sum up exactly how I felt as I tried to return to "normal" life after Natalie's death. Nine-and-a-half months of pure misery, and now at age thirteen our little girl was gone. In a blink, my childhood dream had been shattered. My perfect family was missing an essential part—and so was my heart. This wasn't how it was supposed to be!

In the days and weeks and then months after Natalie's passing, I became proficient at moving my loss into a "box" that allowed me to be fully functional by distracting myself with what needed to be done—whether at work, at home, or at play. The hazard was that I never knew when my "box" might spring a leak, moving me from smiling to crying in a matter of moments. The trigger could be a memory, a picture, a song, a note from a friend, a posting on social media, or an experience I'd had with Natalie.

Our first Christmas without Natalie triggered many such leaks. Christmas had always been her favorite holiday. She listened to Christmas music as early as October, which tortured the rest of us, and loved decorating the tree the day after Thanksgiving. Each Christmas Will and Natalie had been allowed to add an ornament representing something significant from that year until the tree had become a scrapbook of their sports, arts, hobbies, academics, and school portraits.

Throughout the holiday hustle and bustle, Tom and I were intentional in ensuring the true meaning of Christmas—Jesus' birth—was the focus of the season in our household. The kids participated in church programs and picked out gifts for less fortunate children. We went caroling with neighbors, including a stop at the local fire station, where the kids would present brownies to the firefighters, who in turn would graciously invite the children to tour the station and fire engines.

With Natalie gone, the thought of decorating lost its enticement. The weekend when we normally put up decorations had been filled with her funeral and memorial service. Afterwards, the mere thought of pulling out the ornaments that represented so many family memories was beyond us. Our church family had graciously brought us a tree, so Tom and I finally bought a bunch of inexpensive balls and lights to put on it. But it just didn't feel like Christmas, so we decided to book a cruise and leave town for the holiday week. This became our new family tradition, and we now travel as a family every Christmas.

When we returned home from that first cruise, we threw the tree away—decorations and all. We haven't had a big tree since. Our ornaments just represent too many memories. Maybe when we have grandchildren, we will start a new tree tradition.

Recently, I passed a fire engine from our local station on my way to work. Seeing it conjured a vision of Natalie in her green and burgundy coat and hot-pink sweatpants in the back row of caroling kids with her close friend Kathryn by her side. My eyes immediately filled with tears. In fact, I pass the fire station regularly. This just happened to be one of those days when the box sprang a leak.

I also struggled—and sometimes still do—with feelings of guilt and regret over things I wish I'd done differently. As a mother, I'm supposed to protect my children, and I questioned if I'd done my job effectively. Was there something I could have done to save our girl? What if we'd gotten her checked sooner?

I knew letting my thoughts linger in those dark places wasn't helpful. Tom and I had made our decisions based on the information we had at the time. There'd been no overt signs of a problem. In fact, our daughter had just received a positive report during her wellness checkup, so there was no reason to believe her small frame carried a ticking time bomb inside. I reminded myself that none of this had caught God by surprise. He'd allowed the symptoms to manifest themselves when they did for a reason.

There were other regrets I couldn't dismiss so logically. I wished I'd asked Natalie more frequently during those months how she felt emotionally and psychologically. She wasn't shy about sharing her emotions with me when she was well, so I just assumed she'd talk through anything that bothered her. It also seemed at the time that asking someone with cancer how they felt was an insensitive and, frankly, rather stupid question. But looking back, I wondered if Natalie had held things close to her heart because she was concerned about worrying Tom and me.

I also wondered if I should have stayed at the hospital rather than coming home each night. Could she have possibly felt I didn't care enough to seize every opportunity to be with her? Tom and I had always managed our children's conflicting school or sporting events with a "divide and conquer" approach, so we'd handled this situation in the same manner. We didn't want Will feeling neglected with both of us away for extended periods of time, and since Tom could lift and carry her, it made the most sense for him to be there. But reminding myself we'd based our decision on the well-being of both children didn't alleviate my remorse.

I also found myself rehashing painfully the times I'd made Natalie cry during her short life. Not the discipline needed when she disobeyed.

That helped shape her into the young lady she was becoming. But rather the times when I'd made her sad or might have been too harsh. That last Saturday when we'd gone out for dinner with my younger brother and his family, Natalie had started complaining about the choice of restaurant. I'd told her sternly how selfish it was to be changing everyone's plans at the last minute.

In truth, my frame of reference had been past incidents when Natalie tried to control where we went out to eat by pitching a fit, including on one of my birthdays. But then she started to cry, "I just can't eat there! I can't swallow my food!"

Only then did it dawn on me she'd been having difficulty swallowing her food all week. Natalie seldom verbalized her health concerns, but I'm sure she was terrified another thing was going wrong with her body. Unbuckling my seat belt, I climbed into the back seat and held her. Together, we settled on a restaurant where she'd feel comfortable and diverted my family there. Thinking back to her anguished tears, I longed for a do-over.

Still, even when remorse threatened to overwhelm me, I reminded myself that we'd had so many more happy times than sad. All discipline stems from love, and my aim had always been to protect Natalie, instill in her a respect for authority, and help shape her into a godly young woman. Even if there were times I failed, God's Word tells me that Natalie no longer cares about these things. She is happy and free from pain—including any sad memories from her limited time here.

He [God] will wipe every tear from their eyes, and there will be no more death or sorrow or crying or pain. All these things are gone forever. (Revelation 21:4, NLT).

This verse also reminds me of what a loving, caring heavenly Father we have and that, like Natalie's, my own tears, sorrow, and pain will one day be gone forever. After Natalie's death, people often asked me if I was or ever had been angry with God. I can honestly say anger was not an emotion I ever experienced over Natalie's death. I have never blamed God for my heartache. God did not do this to Natalie. Suffering and disease are the consequence of living in a fallen world (Genesis 3).

That said, God does allow suffering to happen, and I believe he particularly allows it if the outcome leads to his glory—more people coming to know him as their Savior, or so that the person enduring the suffering draws closer to him (Romans 5:3-4; 2 Corinthians 1:3-4; James 1:2-4; 1 Peter 1:6-7). I've trusted from the very beginning that God's plan is best. I can't be angry with a God who loves me and has my best interest at heart.

Having said that, I still struggle with understanding the why. Pediatric cancer is rare. Last year approximately eleven thousand new cases of cancer were diagnosed in the United States among children from birth to fourteen years. This is less than 1% of all cancer, and over 85% of such cases experience long-term remission into adulthood.

So why Natalie? When this is so rare, why did God allow her not only to have cancer but to be in the slim percentage of those who don't make it? Couldn't she have served God's kingdom well in a normal lifespan here on earth? When I see or hear reports of child abuse or witness a parent verbally abusing a child in public, I find myself asking again why Natalie was taken when some of these parents don't seem to even want their kids, and we wanted and loved our daughter so much.

I found comfort knowing that Natalie herself never expressed anger over her situation toward God or anyone. In fact, the only time Natalie came close to asking "why me?" was when she'd questioned why God hadn't answered our prayers for healing. In that conversation, she'd brought up another question. "Mommy, why do you think God chose me for this?"

"Chose" was a strange word for a child to use in this context. That she even asked the question implied that she saw her illness as a calling and understood that her loving heavenly Father had a purpose and plan for what she was enduring and that none of it was outside his sovereign control. This trusting acceptance still amazes me.

But though I knew my daughter was alive, happy, and pain-free, and that one day we would be joyously reunited, I also missed her desperately. When my thoughts threatened to linger too long in those dark places, I learned to deliberately take my mind to a more positive place. Sometimes I simply prayed and gave thanks for the time I had with Natalie. I listened to music that spoke to my hurt and offered comfort or reminded me of a happy time. Other times I visited her gravesite, just sitting there to talk to her and God. Sometimes I just looked at pictures, went through her things, or reflected on happy memories. Though all these brought tears, they didn't come from a place of hopelessness but rather *I just plain miss you!*

I would be remiss if I didn't mention Tom as my greatest support throughout this entire journey. I've heard over the years that many marriages fail after the death of a child. I can see why. Losing Natalie took me to an emotional low I'd never experienced. Tom has been my best friend for going on four decades—likely because we balance each other on so many levels. We tend to approach situations from different angles while typically working toward the same end goal. Suffice it to say, the way we processed our grief was also different. So we had to figure out how to best accommodate each other's needs for healing.

In the days immediately following Natalie's death, Tom had a deep need to talk about her, while for me dwelling on past memories was simply too painful at that point. I suggested he reach out to his friends. They graciously connected with him, serving as his outlet until I had more capacity to handle the emotional drain talking about her caused me. I am so grateful to my friends and Tom's who were willing to step into the gap and be there to listen and love on us. Sometimes we both just needed a change of scenery or a chance to laugh or cry with someone who wasn't so close to the situation.

There were other first milestones of Natalie's passing. Easter had always been an important day of celebration for our family. The Easter Bunny brought candy and toys, but our children were taught the significance of the day. They not only heard it at home but also through their Sunday school classes and church activities centered around the holiday.

The last Easter Natalie was alive, I asked her an important question.

"Natalie, why do we celebrate Easter? Is it because the Easter Bunny comes?"

Scrunching up her nose, she responded, "No. The candy and stuff is awesome! But Easter is about when Jesus died on the cross for us and then went up to heaven. Because we believe in him, we also get to go to heaven one day."

My heart was full. Easter is the most important holiday for any Christian, and Natalie understood why. As a Christian parent who had lost a child, Easter became even more meaningful and still is. The resurrection of Jesus Christ means we will see our beautiful girl again one day.

That following November, on Natalie's first birthday since her passing, a group of her friends painted a huge rock that sits in front of the high school she would have one day attended. The basecoat was white. "Happy Birthday, Nat!" and "We miss you!" had been painted against the white in purple. Below those words were Natalie's initials in black with a red heart. Then they'd signed their own names in lime-green.

The high school is on a busy road that I travel going to and from work, so each day I got to see that memorial to my daughter as I drove past. These same friends honored Natalie by repainting the rock in memory of her birthday every year until they graduated from high school and went off to college.

Having outlets to express their grief is one good way to help adolescents process their own feelings. On November 24, 2009—one year after Natalie died—we brought all her close friends together to share their favorite memories and light candles in her honor. We asked them to write notes to Natalie, which we placed in helium balloons and released toward heaven. Throughout high school, her friends banded together in their sadness and found creative outlets to express their pain and loss and to represent her missing presence in their lives.

A more unhappy memorial occurred just two weeks after that anniversary commemoration. On December 8, 2009, our Miniature Dachshund Tucker died unexpectedly at age eight from kidney failure. Losing him would have hurt under any circumstance as he was a dearly loved member of our family. I'd been a work-from-home mom during his puppy days, so Tucker and I had a very close bond. But the sting of his loss was magnified because Natalie's own close bond with him made it feel as though I'd lost another piece of her. Now my perfect dream family of five—four humans and a dog—was down to just three.

In the intensity of my sadness and heartache, I had to consistently caution myself not to allow my loss in this life to overshadow my eternal focus or to fixate on what I was missing instead of maintaining a grateful heart for all of God's love and faithfulness and the way he has blessed us with "beauty for ashes" (Isaiah 61:3). Natalie set an example of claiming the blessings of each day instead of focusing on the negatives. And though it is still a struggle, especially at certain times of the year, I've committed to following her example by starting and ending each day with a prayer of thanksgiving.

In keeping with this, we put a specific verse on Natalie's headstone because it is an accurate representation of who she was and how God expects us to view the situation.

Always be joyful. Never stop praying. Be thankful in all circumstances, for this is God's will for you who belong to Christ Jesus. (1 Thessalonians 5:16-18, NLT)

## HELPS SECTION

# *Words Fitly Spoken*

The Bible says a lot about the power of the tongue and the healing value of words that are wise, gracious, thoughtful, and kind (Proverbs 25:11; 15:23; 16:23; James 3:2, 5-8). But despite good intentions, words meant to console can actually aggravate grief.

**DON'TS: Avoid unsolicited advice or platitudes like the following:**

- "Everything happens for a reason."
- "I know exactly how you feel."
- "Be glad she's no longer suffering."
- "It will all be okay."

**DO'S: Positive things to say include:**

- "Is there a way I can help?"
- "I can't imagine how you must feel. I'm always here to talk if you need me."
- "I'm thinking of you," or "I'm praying for you."
- "I know someone who's been through this with a child. Would you like to speak with them?"

15

# comfort for
# the grieving

"Carry each other's burdens,
and in this way you will fulfill the law of Christ."
—Galatians 6:2 (NIV)

Because so many people provided relief and encouragement to us, I would like to pay it forward and be a resource to those looking for ways to lift the spirits of people walking our same path. I know some are still hesitant to ask me in person for fear of bringing my own pain to the surface—and sometimes it does. So let me here in print share some of the ways people were a great blessing to us—as well as some less helpful responses you might want to avoid.

In the early weeks and months following Natalie's passing, many of our family members, friends, and acquaintances expressed their sympathy and concern. We received lots of notes and cards, which brought great encouragement. It blessed me to read them, and I kept all of them.

At the same time, I was the recipient of platitudes and comments that—much like ill-considered speech during Natalie's illness—came across as pretty insensitive. I sincerely believe these people genuinely wanted to encourage and comfort. But if you want to offer comfort through your words, please listen first, process what you hear, and then weigh your words carefully. Here are some comments I received after Natalie's passing, followed by how they made me feel.

- **"She's in a better place"** or **"You'll see her again one day."** Intellectually, I understand Natalie is in heaven, happy and healed, and I praise God for the resurrection and eternal life, which allows me to see her again. But emotionally that doesn't diminish the pain caused by her physical absence in my life.

- **"She's no longer suffering."** No, she's not, and I am grateful. But our suffering didn't end with her death. We wake up and make it through each day without our daughter.

- **"You should have another child."** A child who has passed away can never be replaced. There are simply no substitutes.

- **"At least you still have Will."** Will is a huge blessing, but I miss my daughter. When someone says that to me, I want to ask them which of their children they can live without.

- **"She's now an angel watching over you."** A sweet thought, but people don't become angels. Angels are separate beings created by God (Hebrews 1:14). I do believe Natalie could be one of the great cloud of witnesses described in Hebrews 12:1.

- **"I'm continuing to pray for Natalie."** There's no need because she's with Jesus. Her eternal destiny became final with her last breath. That's another reason it's so important to teach our kids to love Jesus since there is an age of accountability when children must make the decision to follow Christ of their own free will.

- **"How are you doing?"** My heart has a gaping hole in it, and I'll never be the same. A better question would be, "How are you holding up?" And please don't question the person's answer. I might be okay one moment and not the next. One friend countered every time I answered how I was doing with, "No, really, how are you doing?" I know she meant well, but that aggravated me because if I said I was okay, then I really was.

- **"You've gone back to work too soon."** For me, work was a far more appealing distraction than sitting at home allowing my mind to flood with hurt and my eyes to flood with tears. Allow the person grieving to determine when it's best to re-engage in their normal activities.

- **"You're not crying enough."** Is there a standard amount of crying that constitutes appropriate grieving after the death of a loved-one? I tend to cry when alone because crying in front of people makes them uncomfortable. Some people just aren't criers. It's best to let people grieve in their own way and time. There is no right or wrong way. It's an individual process.

- **"If you weren't handling this so well, people wouldn't assume you're doing well."** Can you ever really be doing well after losing a child? You may get by, but there's always a raw wound. In the first months after Natalie's passing, I had to rely on God to get me out of the bed each day and doses of espresso to keep me awake after sleepless nights.

- **"My ninety-year-old grandma passed away recently, so I understand how you feel."** If you've never lost a child, you have no idea how I feel. Please understand I don't say this to diminish the loss of anyone's loved-one. Death hurts those left behind. But there is a big difference between losing a loved-one who has lived a full life and losing a loved-one at an age that is unnatural.

Some of the above are popular phrases, especially among Christians. Others are insensitive enough anyone taking time to think before speaking should know not to say them. Even years later, I still receive comments that reflect a lack of understanding of the lifelong grieving process the death of a child can bring. One friend texted me requesting prayer for his son's friend who'd been critically injured. He mentioned how deeply this was affecting him even though it wasn't his son who was hurt, then added, "I don't know how you did it. You're a strong person."

The text didn't hurt me because this friend is a kind, compassionate man whose intent was to affirm the strength he sees in me as a Christ-follower. What struck me was his use of the past tense. From his perspective, I'd survived a heart-wrenching tragedy. From my perspective, I was still enduring it and leaning on God to get me through every minute of every day.

Scripture tells us that one reason our loving, compassionate heavenly Father comforts us is so that we in turn know how to comfort others who are suffering:

> Praise be to the God and Father of our Lord Jesus Christ, the Father of compassion and the God of all comfort, **who comforts us in all our troubles, so that we can comfort those in any trouble with the comfort we ourselves receive from God.** (2 Corinthians 1:3-4, NIV)

This is so true, and again I've been guilty of such unthinking comments myself. I now think more carefully before trying to offer words of comfort to those who are hurting. I also remind myself that most people don't set out to say hurtful or offensive things. Knowing that, I typically just smile, thank them for their concern, and ask God to give them wisdom. If the timing and circumstances are right, I may gently share how their words negatively affected me.

I've focused a lot on what not to say. So let me share some things I've found helpful as a mother who has lost a child.

**Just be my friend.** Listen to my stories about Natalie, even if you've heard them over and over. It's one of the few things I have left of her. My stockpile of stories about her won't expand because they stopped at age thirteen. Tell me when you think about her or when a memory comes to mind. Cry with me on my hard days. Hug me on the milestones and anniversaries.

**Listen before you speak**. I find this is where most people struggle. This includes refraining from offering unsolicited counsel that can be construed as insensitive or out of touch. You may think you know how I feel or what I need because you know how much you love your own children. But if you haven't walked in my shoes, then you can't possibly grasp the intensity of my loss.

When you do speak, **be prudent in choosing your words**. Words flowing from a lack of understanding of the depth of pain may totally miss the mark. As Christians, our comfortable go-to is Bible verses. We pick a verse and confidently share it with our grieving friend or loved-one. But for me, certain verses came across as preachy and self-righteous in the context of my grief. Ask God for wisdom on how to approach each situation. Offer comfort. When and if necessary, use words.

**Be present.** Many times, someone's presence alone was sufficient. There was no need to say anything insightful, just to sit there with us. Simple assurances like "I love you …" "I'm hurting for you …" "I'm praying …" "I'm here if you need anything" were a soothing balm. Less was better.

Wondering just what to do or say to someone who has lost a loved-one can be uncomfortable on many levels. Doubts creep in. What if I say the wrong thing? Do the wrong thing? For some, the discomfort can be so paralyzing that they say or do nothing at all. We were fortunate to have so many people supporting us in the weeks following Natalie's passing. But there were others close to me who didn't reach out at all. One friend told me years later that she hadn't reached out because she had no idea what to say. She thought it better not to call than to say the wrong thing.

Please understand how hurtful that can be. The loss hurts badly enough without feeling abandoned when you need your friends the most. It's better to take the risk of saying the wrong thing than appear that you don't care. If a personal conversation is uncomfortable for you, then send a short text or sympathy card. But if you avoid me or say nothing, you can't assume I will know that you care.

On a more practical end, what is the best way to help a family who is wrestling with the recent loss of a loved-one? One suggestion, just as during a time of life-threatening illness, is **offering assistance with day-to-day tasks,** especially in the days immediately after loss. Every hour not spent running errands and performing chores during the grieving process allows for more meaningful family time. Not having to worry about preparing food and buying groceries alleviates a daily burden for the family while providing an outlet for others to help.

In our situation, the same methods of care extended to us during Natalie's illness continued to be a great blessing to us after her death. We had meals delivered to our door every other day for ten months, including the entire time period of Natalie's illness through two weeks following the funeral. Over those same months, our Sunday school class took care of our yard, pruned our trees, and prayed over us. Our family was able to focus on each other rather than worry about daily chores.

Needs will of course vary greatly depending on the family and situation. A sudden, unexpected death will also involve different needs than a long period of caring for a terminally-ill patient. But especially in the first days and weeks after loss, continued offers of assistance will not only be a practical blessing but will let the family know they are not forgotten and abandoned now that the funeral is over.

Again, ask first what would be most helpful to the family. Or check the CaringBridge site or other resource page the family has set up to see if they are still in need of help. Conversely, if there is no further need, posting this to the resource page is also a good idea. Our friends and family were so generous with meals and offers of other help that we had to gratefully and gently let people know about two weeks after the funeral that we no longer needed meals or other help.

Finally, and most of all, **keep praying**. Knowing that others are still sustaining my family and me in prayer is a source of strength and a lifeline when I'm struggling to find my way through my most difficult days. The pain doesn't fade with time. It just takes on a different shape as the memories of what our life was before our daughter became sick mingle with the dashed dreams of what could have been.

When dealing with individuals or families who are going through grief and loss, keep in mind that each journey has its own nuances, as the cause of death and circumstances surrounding it can vary greatly. There are wide disparities in the amount of time loved-ones have to prepare for the possibility of loss. An illness permits the family some time to wrap their heads around the possibility of death while a sudden, unexpected death does not. The loss of a child still living at home affects day-to-day family dynamics differently than a child who had moved out of the home.

Also, people grieve in distinctive ways. I've often heard grief equated to a snowflake or a fingerprint—each unique. There's no one-size-fits-all approach to dealing with or ministering to someone who's experienced this level of grief.

The one constant is that we all hurt. It may manifest itself in different ways at varying degrees at any given time, but the hole left in each of us is very real. We learn to live with the loss, and it becomes a part of who we are. I never would have imagined my daughter would spend "the best years of her life" anywhere but here with us. But I am grateful for the good times we shared together. While I will always miss her and what could have been, I know that what lies ahead for me and Natalie is so much greater than anything I could ever imagine for us here on earth.

## HELPS SECTION

# *Ongoing Support*

One of the most difficult times for a grieving family is when the funeral is over, the sympathy cards and gifts have all been received, extended family and friends have returned to their own lives, and those who have lost a loved-one are presumed to have moved on. But just because life has returned to "normal" doesn't mean grieving stops. Emotional and spiritual support can be as needed and welcomed as at the time of loss. How can you help with the ongoing healing process? To sum it up, **just be a friend:**

- **Listen to our stories.** Even if you've heard them over and over. It's one of the few things we have left of our loved-one.

- **Tell us when you think about our loved-one or when a memory of them comes to mind.** People have told me they don't speak of Natalie out of concern it will upset me or make me sad. The truth is, I get up every morning with the stark reminder she is gone. When someone shares a memory, story, or some way their life was impacted by her, it brings great joy and the assurance she hasn't been forgotten.

- **Cry with us on our hard days.**

- **Acknowledge those "tender" calendar markers.** This includes birthdays, holidays, significant life milestones such as what would have been a graduation, the anniversary of diagnosis or death. You can even offer some people a hug on those days.

- **Speak the loved-one's name.** I've noticed many times that people will refer to "your daughter" when mentioning our girl. My daughter's name is Natalie. It blesses me when people actually refer to her by her name.

- **Keep praying.** When someone loses a loved-one, I am deeply saddened and pray regularly for them. But after a few weeks, the family's loss fades from the forefront of my thoughts unless I am reminded through social media posts or actually see them again. Because I've experienced pain when that happened with Natalie, I now write their name on a sticky note I keep on my desk as a daily reminder to keep praying.

# 16

# moving forward

"But those who trust in the LORD will find new strength.
They will soar high on wings like eagles. They will run
and not grow weary. They will walk and not faint."
—Isaiah 40:31 (NLT)

For over a decade, my new normal has been to wake up and start each day as a mother who has lost one of her children. Not having Natalie as a daily part of our lives is a void that just cannot be filled and an ache that never fully goes away. I've experienced so many emotions, and it remains a day-to-day struggle to try to stay positive.

For one, I wasn't prepared for the emotional challenges associated with returning for the first time to places I'd traveled with Natalie, and I found myself unconsciously avoiding places to prevent a potentially harrowing stroll down memory lane. I saw this happen with one of my favorite cities. Tom and I had taken many trips to Charleston, South Carolina, before we had children, and we'd also visited many times as a family. Natalie and I even traveled there together when I chaperoned her fifth-grade field trip.

After Natalie died, we continued to take family trips to the South Carolina coast each summer. I hadn't realized I'd unconsciously eliminated Charleston from my list of destinations until several years later when we took Will to explore a possible college campus there. As we walked through areas Natalie and I had visited on that field trip, memories began to surface. *We walked down that street. We ate dinner here. We shopped for souvenirs there.* I could actually hear Natalie laughing with her friends, asking to hold my hand, her sweet voice saying, "Mommy, can I have one of these?"

Though my emotions were stirred, it proved a therapeutic trip. I prayed for God's help to move my thoughts from never again experiencing these places with Natalie to focusing on the joy of previous trips. Praise God for his faithfulness! I've now been back to Charleston five times, including 2018 when we attended the wedding of one of Will's best friends.

The same thing happened with Atlanta. We'd visited family there every summer, and since Will and Natalie both loved the Atlanta Braves, we'd take them to see a game. I hadn't realized I'd avoided going back until attending a niece's wedding several years later. Despite some emotional ups and downs, I managed to enjoy the wedding festivities. I've learned that if I make myself go, I can get through it and have crossed off several other such trips with Hawaii still on my list to conquer.

I was also unable to bake cookies for several years because that was something Natalie and I always did together. My breakthrough came one holiday season when my office suggested a cookie day where staff could bring in their favorite cookie to share. I'm sure they'd have been willing to do something else if I'd shared my angst. Instead, I hunkered down in the kitchen Saturday morning baking Christmas cookies, including Natalie's favorite sugar cookie reindeer. I did cry a few times as I baked, but I made it through. I now bake cookies every year.

The start of each school year after Natalie's death was also difficult—especially what would have been her high school and college years. Some of Natalie's friends would ask me to help them choose their classes. It was sweet that they valued my opinion, and I was thankful to help, but it was another painful reminder my daughter was no longer here for me to be helping her through her choices.

When prom season rolled around, I cried every time I saw her friends' beautiful prom photos on social media. One of Natalie's best friends invited me to her high school graduation. This was especially emotional for me as it was the same year Natalie would have graduated. I was doing okay until I glanced back from the activity onstage to where the graduates were seated in alphabetical order. Looking at the names on the program, I counted back to where Yokeley would have been seated among the Ys. I had to quickly turn my attention back to the program to keep my tears from spilling over.

As Natalie's friends went off to college, I wondered what university she'd have attended and what she'd have studied. Most of those friends have now graduated, invoking thoughts of what she'd be doing now. Would she still be pursuing a career as a doctor? Or perhaps she'd be getting married. The wedding invitations have started rolling in, which brings a new set of challenges for my heart.

Birthdays, anniversaries, holidays, and other special occasions remain taxing despite the passage of years. The cemetery where Natalie was laid to rest has a special service each year on Easter. We've only attended once—the first year after Natalie died. But Tom and I still visit her grave each year the weekend before to spruce it up. We lay fresh cedar chips, trim the shrubs, and put fresh flowers in her pots. It may sound silly, but I want her site to look perfect for all of the Easter visitors.

We go back again in the fall to replace the summer sunbaked cedar chips, rake leaves, and lay some small pumpkins—which Natalie loved— on her headstone. God is faithful to bless us with a breeze blowing through and a butterfly fluttering about. It always makes me feel as though Natalie is present with us while we work.

Mother's Day is another bittersweet day. I am grateful for my own mom and for being Will's mother but also saddened I no longer get to be Natalie's mom. The day brings back memories of how much effort Natalie put into making me feel special, and I still have some of the handmade gifts and cards she made for me.

Natalie's birthday is November 1st. I typically drive out to her grave to sit a while—a quiet, reflective time that always helps me with my perspective. Her death anniversary is just a few weeks later on November 24th.

She died the Monday before Thanksgiving and was buried two days after the holiday, so the memories surrounding Thanksgiving bring added distress. Seeing nieces and nephews all together—many now with their own families—makes my own daughter's absence even more glaring and painful. We've spent all but one Thanksgiving alone as a family since she died.

That said, Thanksgiving is also a time I try to express my gratitude to a faithful God who carries me through each day and blessed me with Natalie for thirteen years. I am thankful for all of our friends and family who continue to acknowledge the agony associated with this season and pray for us. I also try to encourage others to remember those who have lost someone close to them. There are many of us who try to smile through the season while fighting back the tears and the anguish.

Conversely, taking Communion has become more special. Prior to Natalie's death, I hadn't realized participating in the Lord's Supper had become more a ritual than a personal, intimate encounter. Now it draws a deep emotional reaction out of me because I understand the gravity of Christ's sacrifice at a much deeper level. Because of what Christ did for the four of us—Tom, Will, Natalie, and me—we will be reunited in heaven one day.

Through all of this season, I worried about how losing his only sibling would impact Will. While not an overtly emotional person, his experience with Natalie had developed in him a deeply empathetic concern for those undergoing suffering as well as an understanding of how an illness can affect the entire family dynamic. In the fall of Will's junior year of high school, Natalie was seven months into her battle with cancer. Having walked this journey with her, Will chose to write his high school research paper on childhood brain tumors to help him better understand what his sister was experiencing. After turning in his project, he searched me out.

"I think I may want to be a doctor," he informed me quietly.

To become a pediatrician had been Natalie's dream. Now it became very clear God was calling Will to this same dream. After graduating from high school in 2010, he attended the University of North Carolina-Chapel

Hill, graduating in 2014. He worked as an EMT and in an asthma clinic until he was accepted into medical school. He graduated from the US Navy Officer Development School as an ensign in July 2018. He is now on full scholarship for medical school, on track to graduate in May 2021, after which he will do three years of residency, then serve at least one term in the Navy.

Having witnessed how Natalie's doctors and nurses cared for her, Will aspires ultimately to offer the same level of care to kids struggling with medical conditions. He shared with me once that when he's having a really stressful time in medical school, "I remind myself that Natalie is the reason I'm doing this."

Will married his beautiful bride, Meagan, on July 15, 2018. I am so deeply thankful for her addition to our family. Meagan's family lives in another state and time zone. So while I'll never have the privilege of being mother of the bride, I was given the privilege of planning Will's wedding and handling logistical decisions typically handled by the bride's family. That God had blessed me beautifully in allowing me this honor was not lost on me. At the same time, being so intimately involved dug deep into a still very raw part of me as the thought kept surfacing that I'd never walk through this process with my own daughter.

Because she had no family close by, Tom and I took Meagan to try on wedding dresses. As she did so, the sales personnel in the bridal shop kept telling me how beautiful my daughter looked. The first few times, I corrected them. After that, I just said, "Thank you."

It was a logical misconception to make since Meagan's features more closely resemble mine than Will's do, and though the wedding preparations were filled with a range of emotions for me, it filled my heart with joy that people thought she was my child. I genuinely loved her like a daughter before the wedding, and now she officially is. No matter how deeply I missed Natalie, Will and Meagan's wedding day was one of the happiest days of my life, above all to see the joy on their faces throughout the proceedings, and I continuously thank God for giving Meagan to our son and family.

Once Will left home for college, Tom went back to work full-time in the logistics industry. As years pass, Tom and I have come to rely more and more on each other since no one else can fully understand our personal loss. Our faith in God has helped both of us draw closer and trust what we cannot see. Thankfully, we don't seem to hit emotional valleys simultaneously. When I'm feeling down about Natalie, Tom offers me an encouraging word and vice versa.

Though we both feel the same intensity of pain, we attach sentimental value to different things. Tom still has a music CD he and Natalie would listen to in the car. I in turn am emotionally attached to our house because Natalie died there—which makes the prospect of downsizing difficult. Friends have invited us to see newly released versions of animated films we watched with Will and Natalie as children. Tom likes to see these because they remind him of happy times. I have no desire to go because it provokes memories of Natalie sitting in my lap, gripping me tightly during the scary scenes.

Still, we acknowledge our differences in how we each grieve and try to be sensitive to each other's needs. Tom listens to the CD when he drives to work and knows he has my blessing to go see the movies without me. I am becoming more open to discussing retirement options that don't include our current residence.

A few other things that were once a mundane part of life continue to be difficult to navigate. Asking whether I have children or how many I have is a common "get to know you" question. But it creates a dilemma for me, and I suspect would make the person asking uncomfortable if I answer honestly. To respond as though Will is my only child for the sake of avoiding awkwardness feels like I'm betraying Natalie's memory by acting as if she didn't exist.

Typically, my solution is to state simply that I have two children, a son who is a young adult and a daughter who passed away from cancer at age thirteen. I try to reassure the person through my tone and demeanor that their having asked is not a problem. Most people offer their sympathy, and we quickly move on. Some want to know more about what happened, and I am willing to share.

# moving forward

Tom and I are probably two of the last people left on the planet who still have a landline. This is because Natalie and Will recorded the greeting on our answering machine fourteen years ago. We love to hear Natalie's voice every time the phone rings and the machine turns on.

When Natalie first passed away, we allowed each of her friends and close family members to take one of her multitude of stuffed animals as a reminder of her. But otherwise her bedroom remained untouched as though time has stood still in that one room of our house. Her clothes still hung in the closet and filled her dresser and chest of drawers. Cabinets of art supplies, stuffed animals, and school projects lined the pale blue walls. Looking at her things conjured up mixed emotions. Joy as I reflected on the time and place, then an immediate emptiness. Those moments are when the sobs would come. I can't count how many times I've stood in her room and cried, *Oh Nat, I miss you! I just miss you!*

Recently, we needed to replace the upstairs carpet. Since we had to move everything out of each room, it seemed a logical time to pack and preserve Natalie's things. Tom and I knew it would be a difficult task, but we both misjudged the emotional impact. There was so much of her in every piece of artwork, knick-knack, and article of clothing. Once we'd moved everything off the floor for the carpet installers, I walked into Natalie's empty room and into her closet. Picking up her favorite black boots from the shelf, I just held them for several moments.

*Kathy, you're torturing yourself!* I told myself as the tears started to pool. Replacing the boots, I walked out from the closet into her room. It looked as bare as when we'd moved in. I could recall Natalie's excitement when she knew this was *her* room and how she'd planned exactly where her furniture would go. Now it felt like all trace of her was gone.

Friends have asked if I put Natalie's things back as they were once the new carpet was installed. The answer is no. Not changing her room over the years was one thing. Putting it all back would have felt like we were creating a shrine. Instead, we sealed up most of her things and placed them in her closet. Then I ordered a new comforter set for the bed that I thought Natalie might have chosen as a young adult woman.

White with light blue accents, it is feminine but not prissy—just like my Nat.

So time passes, but the sadness accompanying Natalie's birthday, anniversaries affiliated with her illness, and holidays is still ever-present. Life continues to be full of milestones for others—graduations, careers, engagements, marriages—that will never be for our Natalie. Even thinking about never getting to see her become a mother makes me incredibly sad. With each new year, the list seems to grow, so I have no doubt there will be more heart-wrenching days ahead.

Sometimes when I hear that someone has passed away, I find myself getting a little jealous. I'm not suicidal. I just long deeply to see my child again. I don't fear death since I know I will be with my Savior in heaven. So I almost yearn for it at times just because I am so ready to be reunited with Natalie. When I hear that a child has been killed in an accident or murdered, I feel grateful I had months to process the possibility of Natalie's death rather than receiving an unexpected knock on the door.

God knows all this. Throughout my ups and downs, he has been my "refuge and strength, always ready to help in times of trouble" (Psalm 46:1, NLT). He consistently reminds me to keep my eyes fixed on him. He convicts me when my perspective starts getting out of whack. He comforts me while I'm sobbing or when I start assigning myself any of the blame for what happened.

He also uses others to encourage me when I need it most. I can't count how many times I've received an encouraging note or call from someone saying, "You were on my mind (or heart) today. I prayed for you." I thank my loving heavenly Father for placing such caring and intentionally compassionate people in my life. I will continue to lean on him on my worst days because he is trustworthy and has proven himself faithful.

HELPS SECTION

# *Getting Through the Tough Days*

Even after a decade, grief over Natalie's loss still at times overwhelms me—and undoubtedly will until I am reunited with my girl in God's presence. But there are certain coping mechanisms that are helpful in getting through the dark times. Here are just a few I've learned to implement when the storm waves threaten to engulf me.

- **Focus on the positive.** When sadness overwhelms, I've learned to deliberately take my mind to a more positive place. Sometimes I simply pray and give thanks for the time I had with Natalie. I listen to uplifting inspirational music that speaks to my hurt and offers comfort or reminds me of a happy time.

- **Take time to consciously remember your loved-one.** I don't want to forget my girl and the good memories of being her mom. Reflecting on happier times by looking through family photo albums, reading notes that she wrote me, or listening to her favorite songs helps me feel connected to her. I visit her gravesite a few times a year, where I just sit and talk to her and God. While I may cry, it also brings a sense of peace and comfort.

- **Create new family traditions.** After Natalie's death, putting up a Christmas tree or doing the Christmas activities we'd done with her was just too painful. We've created a new family tradition of taking a trip together during this time. We still miss our girl but being in a new place with new activities makes it easier to enjoy the holiday without being overwhelmed by sorrow because she isn't with us.

- **Remain in God's Word.** I could not have made it through these last years without the underlying comfort and foundation of trust in God and assurance of God's love for me and my family.

- **Surround yourself with positive, loving people.** Whether friends, colleagues, a loving church family, or your own extended family, spending time with people who care about you is an uplifting antidote to depression and grief.

- **Get involved with a local church.** Our church family, which included our pastor, was unwavering in their love and care for us following Natalie's death. Besides offering a listening ear and encouraging notes, they helped us host our fundraisers by providing the venue, volunteers, and items for auction. Natalie's youth pastor even cooked the spaghetti dinner we served for our first event.

- **Consider grief counseling or support groups.** A pastor can serve as a confidential outlet to help you process your thoughts and feelings from a biblical perspective. Some churches even offer grief support groups or individuals who've been trained to offer comfort to those who are hurting. If your church doesn't provide these services, you may want to seek out a Christian counselor or other such services in your area.

- **Pray** always and constantly. Your heavenly Father knows your heart and will be your greatest comfort and support through your time of grief and healing.

# 17

# losing a young friend

"The LORD is close to the brokenhearted;
he rescues those whose spirits are crushed."
—Psalm 34:18 (NLT)

One thing that brings me sheer joy is when someone shares a memory, story, or some way Natalie touched them—whether through a text, e-mail, call, social media, or in person. These may bring tears to my eyes, but they are happy tears. I love being reminded of my beautiful daughter and her vibrant personality, and I'm so grateful her memory lives on in the person sharing the story.

Over the years, it was both a blessing and truly astonishing how Natalie's friends continued to keep her memory alive. Each January, our church youth group went on a retreat. Natalie had attended the month before she was diagnosed with cancer. Each year after that, the girls she'd roomed with continued to reserve a bed for her at the retreat by putting a "Natalie" sign on it.

Every Labor Day weekend, we'd traveled with our church family to a campsite a few hours away. Will and Natalie always looked forward to these three days packed full of fun, food, and water games with their friends. Several years after Natalie died, one of her church friends brought a cardboard star over to our house that she and other girls from the youth group had made in Natalie's honor, displaying it on the camp's brick wall for the duration of the weekend.

The star was painted light blue with a softball, smiley face, and Natalie's name on it. I still have it in her room, and it brings a smile to think they still missed her after all that time and wanted to honor her that way. The following Halloween, that same group gathered to carve *I<3 NY* (I love Natalie Yokeley) into a pumpkin, then brought it to us to put on our porch.

Natalie's middle-school PTA created a long-term memorial to commemorate our daughter in the school's courtyard. Called Natalie's Corner, it is a beautifully landscaped area surrounding a large rock that holds a plaque with her name, picture, and a comforting scripture etched on it: "Come to me, all you who are weary and burdened and I will give you rest" (Matthew 11:28, NIV). The school invited us to the dedication, which was a very sweet ceremony.

Some friends have honored Natalie's memory in a more permanent way. One of our nephews, who dearly loved his cousin, chose to get a tattoo with Natalie's initials on it as a constant reminder of her. A close friend also got a commemorative tattoo. She shared:

> I chose to add a permanent piece of art to my body to always remind me to be mindful of how I treat others—and how to stay positive when I am feeling defeated. Every time I get a glimpse of the balloon on my back or when people say, "You have a balloon on your back!" I am blessed with the opportunity to remember Natalie and her awesome and fascinating take on life.

One of my own friends from high school raises money each year for pediatric cancer research. For the past few years since we reconnected through social media, she has asked if she can raise money in Natalie's honor. She has raised thousands of dollars through sponsored hiking events that raise funds and awareness for childhood cancer research.

Last year she requested a picture and background information so Natalie could have a commemorative sign on the hiking trail. Tom and I greeted her at the finish line of a twelve-mile hike. Natalie's sign was the last one hikers saw as they left the path. We are so grateful she chooses to remember our daughter each year.

During the first two years after Natalie's death, our own family held two fundraisers with the help of our church family, raising over eighteen thousand dollars for the American Brain Tumor Association. Will helped rally students in the fight against cancer through the University of North Carolina's Relay for Life. He remained heavily involved all four years of his undergraduate studies there, serving as committee chair, vice chair, and finally executive co-chairperson. Through his I HEART NY (Natalie Yokeley) team, he raised almost twenty thousand dollars for the American Cancer Society. This was Will's way of not just remembering his sister but helping others who continue fighting this terrible disease.

One of Natalie's oldest friends, Kathryn, got married not long ago. She'd been like a second daughter to us, and I volunteered to host her bridal shower at our home. When she heard of my offer, she texted, "It'll be so special to have it in your home—like she's there with us too." That brought tears to my eyes since I hadn't even been thinking about Natalie's presence when I volunteered. It meant a lot that one of her dearest friends had.

When Tom and I attended Kathryn's wedding a few months later, her Memory Table included a framed photo of her with Natalie. In a thank you note, Kathryn wrote me, "If we have a baby girl, we plan to name her Natalie." I cried tears of joy as I can think of no greater tribute to my daughter.

That said, not all remembrances of losing a friend to death are positive ones. Family members aren't the only ones who deeply grieve the death of a loved-one. For adolescents, the grief and pain of losing a close friend or classmate can affect them in ways we may not realize. I was surprised and saddened when one of Natalie's dearest friends expressed through tears what she'd been holding inside for over a decade. "For the first time since Natalie died, I feel like she is proud of me!"

This beautiful young lady had just completed an internship with our ministry. She'd spent her summer break from college sharing the gospel and growing in her own walk with God. I'd been actively involved in her life since she and Natalie were in sixth grade. And yet I'd had no idea she felt that way. I'm not sure why she had imposed such an expectation on herself, but I am grateful she felt comfortable enough to share it with me.

Adolescent brains just aren't mature enough to manage this level of emotional distress. These kids walk the same halls without their best buddy. They sit next to the empty desk their friend once occupied. They see the vacant spot at the lunch table that was once filled with chatter and laughter. They miss their favorite cousin at family get-togethers and holiday functions. While the loss can make them stronger in some ways, it can also cause insecurities and even fear, particularly if it is the first time they've lost a friend their age. I've seen how Natalie's death profoundly impacted her friends and cousins.

Eight years after Natalie's passing, her close friend Giovanna described her feelings:

Natalie's death had a huge impact on my life. I think that it affected me in both good and bad ways. I really wish I could have been able to spend more time with Nat when she was here, especially while she was sick. Because I regret not spending that time with her, I think that it made me a more intentional person. I reach out to the people I care about and make sure to spend as much time as I can with them. I think that Nat's death made me become more emotionally attached to people, but it also has made me a person who does not open up easily. I constantly find myself putting up walls when I begin to get close to someone because I fear losing someone I love again.

Amanda, another friend from both church and school, shared these comments:

# losing a young friend

After losing Nat, I try my hardest to not take any days for granted or people in my life. I am a very emotional and loving person to my friends and family. I probably go a little overboard at times, but I am terrified to lose anyone close to me … I am content with the years I got to spend with Nat. I do miss her every day, but I am glad for the thirteen years we had as friends. I prefer that over not knowing her at all.

Many of Natalie's friends have expressed their thoughts on social media. On her twenty-fourth birthday, her best friend Sydney shared an online "memory" post from two years prior:

Happy Birthday to my best friend Natalie! I wish you could be here to celebrate down here on earth, but God's plans are kind of different, and I bet you were having so much fun up there. I miss you every day … You have made me see life through a different perspective. You keep me positive when things get stressful, and you always remind me to be appreciative of a healthy body and mind … P.S. You've kept me out of a lot of dumb situations by me asking myself, "What would Nat do?" Earth will never be the same, but you sure did change me. Love you so!

The updated caption from her post added:

Always a great memory when I had the best friend who allowed me to be myself and was ready to adventure and do anything with me! This year Nat has really been watching over me. I hope you have a great 24th birthday from Heaven. Love you so much, Nat.

So how can we help young people who are going through deep grief and trauma over the loss of a friend? One vital outlet is simply providing someone they can talk to about their friend. One of Natalie's childhood friends called Tom and me distraught on the anniversary of her death during the friend's first year away at college.

"I realize my mom has always sheltered me from thinking about this day," she told us through tears. She recounted how she'd fallen apart earlier in the day and even scared some poor young man in her dormitory elevator with her uncontrollable sobbing. This same young lady shared her regrets over not visiting Natalie when she was sick.

"I was afraid," she said. "I didn't want to catch cancer."

Somehow, she'd been under the impression that cancer was contagious. Once Natalie passed away, she felt guilt over not having visited her more. She hadn't been prepared for the possibility that Natalie would actually die. The thought had simply never crossed her young mind. So she'd been completely devastated when it happened.

Sometimes adolescent feelings of loss may run deeper than we feel equipped to handle. One of our nephews said, "I wish it was me and not Natalie." Another teenage friend thankfully sought out professional counseling.

From a spiritual perspective, even if teenagers have been raised in church, we can't assume they will naturally lean on God to help them cope with their loss. One church teen who was a friend of our kids was angry at God for letting Natalie die. A few years later, he confessed at a youth retreat that he'd wanted no part of God after her death. Thankfully, he stayed connected to his youth group, and this particular retreat helped him break through.

On the last night of the retreat, he said to Will, "I've watched how you've handled Natalie's death. If you aren't angry at God, then I shouldn't be either."

These kids will also hold on to the only tangible pieces they have left of their friend. Giovanna has continued to be a part of our family since Natalie's passing and views Will as a brother. Some years back, she accompanied us to Will's college, where he was participating in and I was keynoting for a Relay for Life event for the American Cancer

Society. As she climbed into her bed at the hotel where we were staying, I noticed she still had the stuffed animal I'd given her from Natalie's room.

"I sleep with it every night," she told us. Giovanna also kept the valentine Natalie made for her when she was in the hospital the week of her cancer diagnosis. She recently sent me a picture of it.

Some time ago while helping my sister move, my mother was cleaning out my niece Bailey's closet. She was about to toss out a bag full of clothes when Bailey stopped her. "No, those are Natalie's clothes!"

Since Bailey was Natalie's favorite cousin, I'd given her some of Natalie's unworn or slightly worn clothes right after Natalie passed. Bailey had kept those clothes in a bag in the back of her closet for over a decade, and she still doesn't want to part with them.

Many of Natalie's friends still want to interact with our family. I imagine it's because we are the only part of Natalie left for them to hold on to. One day a couple of years after Natalie died, Giovanna looked at me and smiled. "You're a lot like Natalie."

That's probably why she likes being around me. Tom and I treasure the moments we get to spend with each of Nat's friends, and we love to hear what's happening in their lives. Occasionally, they share memories of Natalie and how she influenced who they are today. It is therapeutic for me, and I suspect it is for them as well.

I continue to pray for each of these friends of Natalie's regularly, and I am hopeful they will always feel comfortable sharing with us. I try to be intentional about being available for any of them who need a listening ear or may need for me to simply serve in Natalie's role as their cheerleader.

## HELPS SECTION

# *Support for Mourning Friends*

Immediate family aren't the only ones who are in pain over losing a loved-one to a terminal illness. Support for grieving friends is very important, especially when dealing with children. Before Natalie, our family had never known any child with a terminal illness, nor had most of her friends and their families. So I'm sure their parents struggled with how to talk with their children about what was happening to their friend. But ignoring it just makes matters worse. Here are some useful pointers in dealing with mourning young friends we learned from experience.

- **Listen when they need to talk about their friend.** If they don't bring it up, ask them questions to see how they are doing.

- **Encourage them to interact with and visit their sick friend** if they feel comfortable. After she passed away, some of Natalie's friends deeply regretted not having spent more time with her.

- **Encourage them to write notes** to their sick family member or friend.

- **Provide outlets to express their grief.** This can help adolescents in particular to process their feelings. Having someone beyond parents to talk to about their friends can also be an outlet, whether a counselor, youth leader, or pastor with whom they feel comfortable discussing their feelings or asking spiritual questions.

- **Host a gathering** where friends of the deceased can come together to share their feelings and memories.

- **Encourage them to band together in finding creative outlets** to express their pain and acknowledge their friend's missing presence in their lives. This can include creating a memorial or other expression of love in memory of their friend.

- **Encourage professional counseling if need be.** Sometimes feelings may run deeper than parents feel equipped to handle. In these cases, for immediate concerns over the depth of despair, contact the National Suicide Prevention Lifeline at 1-800-273-8255.

- **Acknowledge that it's okay to hold onto the only tangible pieces they have left of their friend.** Be understanding when they don't want to throw something out.

- **Stay in touch with the deceased friend's family** if this helps with healing, as it likely offers comfort to the family as well.

- **Pray for them.**

18

# natalie's legacy

"Live wisely among those who are not believers,
and make the most of every opportunity. Let your
conversation be gracious and attractive so that you
will have the right response for everyone."
—Colossians 4:5-6 (NLT)

Natalie did so much to point others to Jesus during her thirteen short years. I never fully understood the extent of her influence on others until after she passed away. She didn't just trust Jesus when things were going well but lived out her faith even on her worst days. It isn't the wheelchair, loss of hair, or inability to do normal adolescent things people remember about her but her inner strength, kindness toward others, and desire to live every day to the fullest no matter the circumstance.

One of Natalie's friends created a video from photos of her cancer journey, which she then posted online. Almost every photo shows her smiling—and on many of those days there wasn't much to smile about! While I doubt anyone could describe her as happy during this season, her countenance showed what was inside of her—joy.

Joy can actually become strongest when the storms come because storms lead to a deeper trust in God. Natalie was proof of this. Even when life threw her the unexpected curveball called cancer, she strove to rise above her circumstances and find joy in the small wins and through her relationships with family, friends, and her Savior Jesus Christ.

Sometime after this video was posted, we received a package from Italy. Inside we found a silk flower, stuffed bear, and a letter written in Italian. Using an online program to translate the letter, we discovered that it was sent by an Italian woman who had seen the video of Natalie online and wanted to express her sympathy for our loss.

"Her smile and sweetness have left an indelible mark on my heart," she wrote, then went on to ask if we would please put the items in the box on Natalie's grave. Three years after her death, the joy Natalie exuded even in the midst of brutal suffering had touched someone she'd never met in a country five thousand miles away.

We're also thankful for how God has continued to use Natalie's faith and knowledge of his Word through some of the artwork she created during her extended hospital stay. A number of the Bible verses she illustrated have been printed to be used as notecards to inspire others who are sick or in need of encouragement. On a business trip to the UK several years ago, I brought a gift for the teenage daughter of a colleague there. She was battling health issues and had been recently hospitalized, so I placed a package of Natalie's scripture notecards in her gift bag. I recently received a request from this young lady, now in college, for more of Natalie's cards.

"I love to use them as thank you cards or notelets for people who aren't Christians, and I'm starting to run out," she wrote. My daughter is sharing God's love through her artwork in a country she never set foot in!

God has even used Natalie to bring encouragement and healing through dreams and visions. After Natalie became close friends with Giovanna during their sixth-grade year, Giovanna wanted to get involved in a church youth group like Natalie's, but her mother was not interested in changing churches. After Natalie passed away, I took Giovanna out to dinner for her birthday. During dinner, Giovanna told me about a dream she'd had on New Year's Eve just a few weeks after Natalie died. In her dream, Natalie had come back to school to spend the afternoon with Giovanna.

"I was really bummed I didn't get the chance to say goodbye or tell Natalie how much she'd changed my life and how much I loved her," Giovanna said. "In the dream, I got to tell her everything I didn't get to tell her when she was here."

After they'd finished talking, Natalie wished Giovanna a Happy New Year and told her everything was going to be okay. Giving Giovanna a hug, she promised that Giovanna would see her again soon. Giovanna awoke more at peace with Natalie's passing but also more determined to be involved in a youth group. She brought the subject up again with her mother, but her mother was adamant about not changing churches.

A few months later, Giovanna's mother had a dream. She knew who Natalie was but had never met her. In her dream, Natalie was standing next to Jesus with a cross in her hands. Walking over to Giovanna's mother, she handed her the cross and said, "This is for you."

Giovanna's mother woke up with the desire to find a different church. The church they ended up attending had a good youth group, and Giovanna accepted Christ as her Lord and Savior. She will be in heaven one day because Natalie shared what gave meaning to her own life and because Jesus loved a hurting thirteen-year-old girl so much that he drew her to himself through a dream about my daughter. I wholeheartedly believe there will be others in heaven as well who are there because of Natalie.

I also received a call some years ago from the young man who'd led the praise and worship at Natalie's funeral. He'd grown up in our church and was married with a young daughter of his own. Several months earlier, his wife had miscarried their second child, a boy whom they'd decided to name Noah. His wife had been distraught for months over the loss of Noah, and he had been unable to comfort her.

Then one morning when he got up, he found his wife in the kitchen whistling and in a great mood. She told him she'd had a dream that had given her the peace she'd been seeking. In the dream, she'd seen a young girl holding Noah's hand. The girl told her, "Noah's fine. He's with me and Jesus. We're at Disney World."

When this young man asked his wife what the girl looked like, she described a young girl perhaps eleven or so years old with brown hair and freckles. Taken aback, he asked, "Do you remember her name?"

His wife stood there for a moment trying to recall, then finally said, "It was 'Yoke' or something like that."

"Yokeley?" he asked. "Natalie Yokeley?"

"Yes, that's it!" she exclaimed.

The young husband had called to tell me that story with the hope it would bring comfort and peace. And it did. But what I found most astonishing was that this was the second time since Natalie's death that God had used her along with the world-renowned amusement park to bring comfort to someone grieving the loss of a child. The first time it was me!

I'd attended the funeral of a friend's four-year-old granddaughter who'd also lost her battle with a brain tumor. That night while lying in bed restless and grieving, I had a vision of a particular ride at Disney World where you fly over the city of London, viewing all of the beautiful, bright lights of the city from above. At that moment, I distinctly heard Natalie's voice say, "Mommy. Brooklyn's okay. She's with me. This is what we see *every* day."

Though sad over the death of yet another child from cancer, I felt a sense of peace that Natalie was telling me they were in heaven and had such a magnificent view. How wonderful for God to take what we regard in our finite minds as one of the happiest places on Earth for our children and use it to give us a picture of what heaven is like for them. It shows God's love and compassion toward us that he'd use such a relatable experience to offer us peace, allowing us to wrap our human brains around the sheer joy our loved-ones must be experiencing in the presence of Christ.

One day about six years after Natalie died, I received a call from the young wife of a colleague. They had graciously provided dinner for our family a few times during Natalie's illness but had never met her personally. The woman explained that she'd been struggling with a chronic auto-immune disorder since childhood. Having children had intensified her illness, and now she'd been diagnosed with Lyme Disease.

The day she called, she'd just left the doctor's office and was feeling pretty discouraged. As she drove, she asked God, "Are you going to heal me of this? Are you going to let me die?"

At that moment, she saw Natalie in the passenger seat of her car. She was so startled she pulled over to the side of the road. Natalie looked around nineteen with long, dark hair and freckles. Though the woman had never met her, she felt as if she'd known her all of her life. In cheerleader mode, Natalie told the woman, "Go! Don't you know that Jesus is your healer?"

"But you died!" the woman said with astonishment.

"But I'm with Jesus, and he's your healer," Natalie responded. "Run! Finish the race!"

It felt to the young woman as if she and Natalie were in a relay race. Natalie had run the first leg and was now passing the baton off to her. She shared with me that she'd never felt so encouraged. As her cheerleader, Natalie was reminding her that Jesus is her healer and she must trust and push forward.

I was awed, not only at how God had used Natalie to encourage this young woman but that when she'd called to share this story, it was only a few months shy of Natalie's nineteenth birthday. I am sure there are more stories like these. It encourages me to know Natalie is being used in supernatural ways to draw others to Christ and to bring emotional healing and comfort.

Others have expressed their sentiments in writing. A close family friend wrote a poem about Natalie four months after her passing.

### I Miss Her

*I miss her hugs.*
*Those were such sweet, sweet hugs.*
*I miss her laugh and her smile.*
*They warmed my heart all the while.*
*I miss her drawings and her writing*
*Describing the fight she was fighting.*

# natalie's legacy

*I miss her wit and humorous disdain.*
*It was her way of shielding us from the pain.*
*I miss her faith and her witness, which was her calling.*
*No telling how many souls she kept from falling.*
*I know she is healed and with the Father, as was his will,*
*But I miss her, I miss her still.*

Natalie's sixth-grade electives teacher still uses her as an example when his students make excuses for not doing their work. One of his comments on my Facebook page reads: "Remembering Natalie motivates me to continue working with students even when I hit a rough patch."

He is currently the senior counselor at a high school and in charge of the local scholarship process. Earlier this year, he sent us a message stating his desire to create a needs-based scholarship in Natalie's name for students wishing to go to college and enter into a helping profession. What a gift to our family! We were thrilled to award the Natalie Yokeley Memorial Scholarship to its first recipient last spring.

A colleague who has been enduring poor health shared recently that at a low point he pulled out Natalie's scripture note cards. He was reminded that if the apostle Paul could praise God while in prison and Natalie could praise God in the midst of cancer, he should praise God too.

Have you ever hugged someone, then realized your clothing smelled like that person's perfume or after-shave? When Natalie was a toddler, Tom would lie down with her at bedtime until she fell asleep. Consequently, her linens and the small blanket she slept with absorbed his scent to the point that when I washed her bedclothes, she'd have a meltdown, crying, "My blanket doesn't smell like Daddy!"

The more we genuinely interact with Christ and seek to know him, the more his aroma should rub off on us. Natalie spent time in God's Word, in prayer, in worship, and encouraged others to seek him. As a result, she "smelled" like Jesus. People who knew her would agree it was obvious she'd been in his presence. That was her legacy. I pray it will be mine as well!

# 19

# eternal
# perspective

"Now is your time of grief,
but I will see you again and you will rejoice,
and no one will take away your joy."
—John 16:22, NIV

Someone asked me recently if Natalie's death has gotten any easier to bear. I'm learning over time to cope better with my loss, but I wouldn't say it's easier. Most days I'm able to talk about Natalie without getting emotional, but there are days when I can't do so without tearing up or crying. I still have moments where the grief from deep within wells up without any notice, leaving me sobbing until it goes away as quickly as it came.

I still miss having my daughter physically present in my life, and I think about her every single day. I often wonder what she'd look like now. I have even toyed with getting one of those police sketches where they age the picture of a child. I envision her as a beautiful, strong, lively young lady. I imagine the shopping trips we'd enjoy together. I experience nostalgia and sadness when I pass by the girl's department in certain stores.

I also wonder what kind of relationship Natalie and Will would have had as adults. They were so close as kids. I know Will still misses Natalie being there for special milestones like his wedding day and mourns the loss of friendship she and Meagan would have had. I wonder at times if Jesus has bruised ribs from Natalie nudging him to say, "Look at my Will!"

I still have so much love in my heart for both my children. Author Franchesca Cox captures my feelings beautifully: "A mother is not defined by the number of children you can see, but by the love she holds in her heart."[5]

My thoughts about Will constantly change as he continues to grow. And though Natalie is no longer physically present, my thoughts about her change as well. When she first passed away, it was like her being away on a trip. Then reality set in that she was gone forever and that our daily routine and family dynamic were permanently altered. While I trust God and his plan for Natalie, I frequently think about what I no longer have and long for those days of being her mom.

I am so grateful God encourages me when I least expect it. I see girls post on social media about how close they are with their mothers, even that they consider their mom to be their best friend. I have often wondered if Natalie would have felt the same way about me. Then just recently I found a picture she'd drawn of the two of us holding hands. At the top, she'd written, "Best Friends Forever." I could not stop saying thank you to God for caring enough to show me that Natalie already considered me her best friend while she was still with me.

In moments when my mind lingers on what I'm missing, I try to redirect my thoughts to where Natalie is now. Even if she had survived the cancer, her long-term prognosis would have entailed serious physical limitations and chronic illness. Instead, she's no longer experiencing disease, pain, or sadness. She will never face broken relationships, job loss, financial concerns, and many of the other hardships we experience in life.

If my thoughts of Natalie are constantly changing, I can say with absolute certainty that her death has changed me. I am a different person now. Losing Natalie has opened my mind in many ways, helping me to better understand what's important in life and to view others with more grace.

It has also shifted my priorities. For most of my life, I was always the planner with a "to do" list. Now I pray over what God has for me and only choose activities I feel he is directing.

My free time and vacations are also more relaxed because I've learned to be present in the moment rather than looking too far ahead. I've learned to rest. The first time I experienced a real vacation was after Natalie died. Tom and I were on a cruise with no expectations or plans. We set no alarms. When we woke up, we ate a leisurely breakfast, then figured the rest out as the day progressed. It dawned on me that I'd always had every vacation totally mapped out. Now for once I was just enjoying my family and the rest. This became my new normal.

Losing Natalie has also created some fences around my heart to protect me from further heartache. I used to hang out with almost anyone who asked me. Now I am more intentional about my social interactions and who I allow into my personal space. I want to spend my available free time with people I enjoy being with—people who are uplifting and inspiring.

That said, I have a deeper appreciation for people who open up their hearts to me, and I want them to leave our encounter knowing I truly care. I try not to offer superfluous advice but to listen, encourage, and pray. I am more faithful now when people ask me to pray because I've seen firsthand the power of prayer to sustain us through difficult situations. I am also more intentional in following up on the situation since specific needs may change along the way. One week, prayer might be needed on behalf of the doctors for wisdom and guidance in diagnosis while the next it could be adverse reactions to medications.

As the analytical planner type, I used to jump right into "fixer" mode when I listened to people's problems or stories. Many times, I was thinking about what I wanted to say before they even finished. I was prone to turn a story back to something in my own life because I thought that showed empathy. Since Natalie's illness and death, I've learned there are things I can't fix—only God can. I've realized most people don't need to hear a story from my life because it doesn't change their plight. They just need a listening ear, a shoulder to cry on, or me to pray with them.

Sometimes I will offer counsel or, if they ask, share what God has shown me throughout my own journey of pain.

Another change is in my quiet time with God. I've enjoyed studying God's Word for decades. But in the days and years since Natalie's death, it feels richer and I experience a greater intimacy with God. Maybe it's a by-product of how much I trust God and his love for me. Maybe I need to hear him speak to me even more now than before. Whatever the reason, I'll take it. I crave it.

Natalie's death has changed my perspective on life as well. I now see situations through an altered lens. I try to separate the petty from the important. I tend to weigh situations against my loss, and many times this helps me weed through the minutiae. But I also have to guard against being judgmental about someone else's suffering if I perceive it as a lesser measure of severity than my own suffering. *Are you kidding me? My daughter died! What you're going through isn't suffering!* When such thoughts flood my mind, I have to repent and be intentional about responding kindly.

But though I may be different now, God never changes. His love and faithfulness remain abundant. After Natalie died, a friend commented, "You carried Natalie for the first nine months, and Tom carried her for the last nine months." A kindly intended statement but not accurate. God carried our little girl for thirteen years, and he is still carrying her and us today.

I mentioned before how much I love the ocean in all its beauty and power and even the turbulent violence of its tempests so long as I can watch from a safe shelter. But it is equally awe-inspiring to observe the calm that settles over the sea once a storm has passed. As I walk along the shoreline, scattered debris offers proof of the storm's fury. Its impact leaves behind a landscape that has been altered in devastating but also beautiful ways. Shattered rock forms fascinatingly intricate sculptures. Washed-away sand becomes a crystal-clear tide pool filled with treasures. Opalescent shells churned up from the ocean depths glint rainbow hues in the sunlight.

As with the shoreline, the storm of Natalie's illness and death has definitely left debris in its wake. The landscape of my life has been forever altered in devastating but sometimes beautiful ways. I never expected to bury a child. It is not a natural progression of life for parents to outlive their children, and it will always be painful to think about what could have been. While time has softened the rawness of my wound, the scar will always be there.

But I've also discovered a newfound beauty in God's utter faithfulness in both good times and hard. He helps me keep my eyes fixed on him. He turns my focus to the blessings stemming from Natalie's death rather than getting caught up in the heartache and loss. He is my firm foundation and promises to strengthen me, help me, and uphold me with his righteous right hand (Isaiah 41:10) as I survive each day without one of the most important people in my life.

Another beauty the storm has left behind is a deepened, strengthened closeness as a family. We understand that life is fragile and there are no guarantees tomorrow will come. We still hurt and grieve together and will never fully understand this side of heaven why God felt he could accomplish more for his kingdom through Natalie's death than through her life. I struggle some days more than others to accept that this was God's choice and plan for our girl.

But when I struggle, I never doubt that God loves me and my family. God has been our refuge in the storm, and our faith in him has helped us weather even the darkest, most tempestuous days. As scripture promises, "faith shows the reality of what we hope for; it is the evidence of things we cannot see" (Hebrews 11:1, NLT). If we cannot see clearly now, one day we will know and understand (1 Corinthians 13:12). That will be the day we are reunited with our girl in the loving presence of our Lord and Savior Jesus Christ.

I suspect I will always carry an underlying tinge of sadness even during my happiest days. I will wonder how much better or more fun each experience might be with my girl as a part of it. But what I mostly feel is gratitude. I'm grateful to have been Natalie's mom for even a short time. That's a gift from God which will never be taken away.

# epilogue

# wedding
# reservation

"As a young man marries a young woman,
so will your Builder marry you; as a bridegroom rejoices
over his bride, so will your God rejoice over you."
—Isaiah 62:5, NIV

This story began with a wedding. A beautiful, joyous occasion that was marred only by the absence of a loved-one who should have been there. But though my only son is now married and I will never be mother of the bride for my only daughter, Will and Meagan's wedding is not the last in which I will be a participant. One day I will be blessed to be part of the most beautiful wedding this universe has ever known—the long-awaited marriage of the Lamb, the Lord Jesus Christ, and his bride, the church (Ephesians 5:25-32). The apostle John describes this upcoming event for us in the book of Revelation:

> Then I heard again what sounded like the shout of a vast crowd or the roar of mighty ocean waves or the crash of loud thunder: "Praise the Lord! For the Lord our God, the Almighty, reigns. Let us be glad and rejoice, and let us give honor to him. For the time has come for the wedding feast of the Lamb, and his bride has prepared

herself. She has been given the finest of pure white linen to wear." For the fine linen represents the good deeds of God's holy people. And the angel said to me, "Write this: Blessed are those who are invited to the wedding feast of the Lamb." And he added, "These are true words that come from God." (Revelation 19:6-9, NLT)

This occasion will be even more beautiful because Tom, Will, Meagan, *and* our precious Natalie will also be there. And this time there will be no tears. No need for a Memory Table. I'll have no desire to be distracted from painful memories. Our family will be whole again. It will be a time of complete joy.

I have a reservation at this wedding feast because I have accepted Jesus Christ as my Lord and Savior and my name is written in the Lamb's Book of Life (Revelation 21:27). In fact, every human being on this planet has an open invitation to attend this wedding as part of the bride of Christ if they have professed Jesus as Lord and Savior.

But while our family reserved a seat for Natalie at Will's wedding, *she* had to make her own personal reservation in the Lamb's Book of Life to secure her invitation to this marriage of the Lamb. We all did. Though our reunion may be years and even decades away, Tom, Will, Meagan, and I have absolute assurance we will be joining Natalie at this wedding feast and spending eternity together in heaven.

Unfortunately, there will be others we love who are absent from this wedding because they didn't surrender their lives to Christ. If their names are not written in the Lamb's Book of Life, they will be missing from the guest list.

Will you be at the wedding feast? Have you made your reservation? No one can make it for you. This reservation comes with the cost of a commitment from you:

Then he [Jesus] said to the crowd, "If any of you wants to be my follower, you must give up your own way, take up your cross daily, and follow me." (Luke 9:23, NLT)

# wedding reservation

If you haven't yet, you can make your reservation today. There's plenty of space but a restricted amount of time, as the apostle Paul warns us:

This is all the more urgent, for you know how late it is; time is running out. Wake up, for our salvation is nearer now than when we first believed. (Romans 13:11, NLT)

Life offers no guarantees. No one knows when they will take their last breath. But God does offer a guarantee. He is offering all of us an opportunity to enter into a relationship with his Son Jesus Christ and secure our place with him in eternity:

For this is how God loved the world: He gave his one and only Son, so that everyone who believes in him will not perish but have eternal life. (John 3:16, NLT)

Would you like to be forgiven of your sins and filled with a sense of peace and joy that you've never experienced before? The things of this world will always leave you empty, but Jesus "satisfies the longing soul, and fills the hungry soul with goodness" (Psalm 107:9, NKJV).

Allow Jesus to become the ruler of your life. If you aren't sure how, you can find out on page 159. You'll never regret it.

I hope to see you at the wedding!

# addendum

# God's plan
# for you

A re you yearning for change in your life? Let Jesus be your source of peace and hope. Allow him to be your joy. "…He will neither fail you nor abandon you" (Deuteronomy 31:6, NLT). Here's how you can experience the "rich and satisfying life" God has for you (John 10:10) and spend eternity in his presence.

- **Confess your sin.** "For everyone has sinned; we all fall short of God's glorious standard" (Romans 3:23, NLT).

- **Sin leads to death, but we can receive eternal life as a free gift.** "For the wages of sin is death, but the free gift of God is eternal life through Christ Jesus our Lord" (Romans 6:23, NLT).

- **God loves us even while we sin.** "But God showed his great love for us by sending Christ to die for us while we were still sinners" (Romans 5:8, NLT).

- **Accept Jesus as your Lord and Savior.** "If you openly declare that Jesus is Lord and believe in your heart that God raised him from the dead, you will be saved. For it is by believing in your heart that you are made right with God, and it is by openly declaring your faith that you are saved" (Romans 10:9-10, NLT).

- **Rejoice that your salvation is now assured.** "Everyone who calls on the name of the LORD will be saved" (Romans 10:13, NLT).

If you aren't sure how to pray to receive Jesus as your Savior, use the following example.

"Dear God, I know I'm a sinner, and I ask for your forgiveness. I believe Jesus Christ is your Son, that he died for my sin, and that you raised him to life. I want to turn from my sin and to trust and follow Jesus as my Lord and Savior. I pray this in Jesus' Name. Amen."

# notes

*Chapter 4*

1. Gary D. Chapman, *The 5 Love Languages* (Northfield Pub., 2015), 55.

*Chapter 6*

2. Henry Blackaby, Richard Blackaby and Claude King, *Experiencing God: Knowing and Doing the Will of God* (Nashville: B&H Publishing Group, 2008), 21.

*Chapter 11*

3. *The Complete Works of C. H. Spurgeon, Volume 2: Sermons 54-106,* (Delmarva Publications, Inc, 2015), 233, accessed March 10, 2019, https://www.spurgeon .org/resource-library/sermons/a-bottle-in-the-smoke#flipbook/.

*Chapter 12*

4. David Johnson, *Voice of Beauty* (Charleston: Advantage Media Group, 2009), 99.

*Chapter 19*

5. Franchesca Cox, *Facets of Grief: A creative workbook for grieving mothers* (Create Space Publishing, 2017), 109

Made in the USA
Monee, IL
28 March 2021